I0760205

THE LOUISIANA URBAN GARDENER

THE LOUISIANA URBAN GARDENER

A Beginner's Guide to Growing Vegetables and Herbs

KATHRYN K. FONTENOT

LOUISIANA STATE UNIVERSITY PRESS
BATON ROUGE

Published by Louisiana State University Press
lsupress.org

Second printing, 2022

Designer: Laura Roubique Gleason
Typefaces: Sentinel Book (text); Harman (display)
Printer and binder: Sheridan Books

Unless otherwise credited, all photographs were taken by the author.

Library of Congress Cataloging-in-Publication Data

Names: Fontenot, Kathryn K., 1981– author.
Title: The Louisiana urban gardener : a beginner's guide to growing vegetables and herbs / Kathryn K. Fontenot.
Description: Baton Rouge : Louisiana State University Press, 2018. | Includes index.
Identifiers: LCCN 2017005922 | ISBN 978-0-8071-6679-6 (cloth : alk. paper)
Subjects: LCSH: Gardening—Louisiana. | Vegetable gardening—Louisiana. | Herb gardening—Louisiana.
Classification: LCC SB453.2.L8 F66 2018 | DDC 635.09763—dc23
LC record available at https://lccn.loc.gov/2017005922

This book is for all those who love to garden, especially my children. Jacob, eight years old, has already grown many gardens, and Charlotte, two years old, will grow many to come.

This book is also dedicated to my parents, Marlys and Kenneth Karsh, and my husband, Dexter Fontenot, also wonderful gardeners.

CONTENTS

ACKNOWLEDGMENTS

Much of the knowledge and garden experience I share in this book I owe to my many mentors: Dr. Joe Kuban, Dr. Jimmy Boudreaux, Dr. Charlie Johnson, Mr. Bob Mirabello, Dr. Edward Bush, Dr. Allen Owings, Dr. Jeff Kuehny, Dr. Don LaBonte, Dr. David Himelrick, Dr. Carl Motsenbocker, Dr. James McCrimmon, Dr. Ron Strahan, Dr. Jeff Beasley, Dr. David Picha, Mr. Dan Gill, and the late Dr. Don Ferrin. I cannot thank each of these individuals enough for helping me. I am also grateful to every vegetable producer in Louisiana. Visiting their farms and working with them on field trials has been a very rewarding experience. They teach me so much every day.

THE LOUISIANA URBAN GARDENER

INTRODUCTION
GARDENING IN LOUISIANA

Many joke that rather than the traditional seasons, the four seasons in Louisiana are Carnival, Crawfish, Football, and Hurricane. While our weather is not often bragged about, it is excellent for one thing—gardening. Louisianans are blessed with a moderate climate enabling us to garden year-round. Year-round gardening creates challenges, such as insects and disease. Gardeners must stay on their toes as nothing stays the same from season to season. However, very few activities can compete with the magic of watching a seedling push its way through the soil to eventually flourish into something delicious to eat. The taste of a fresh homegrown tomato or slice of cucumber puts a smile on every gardener's face. This book will guide beginning gardeners, from planning the garden to enjoying the harvest. With a little effort and patience, anyone can connect to nature and truly enjoy their backyard garden.

Who's Growing?

One of the nicest aspects of gardening is that absolutely anyone can do it. My son's first potato crop was planted in our backyard just after he started walking. Many children begin gardening around the age of three or four years old. With a little guidance from teachers and volunteers, children in childcare centers across the state of Louisiana are successfully cultivating fall and spring gardens. Through this simple activity, they are developing not only a love for nature but also a palate for something other than a prepackaged snack. Gardening is also popular among elementary, middle, and high school students. Boys and girls alike are taking part in this activity that many will continue throughout their working life and well into retirement.

A favorite stat among those working in the agriculture sector is that the average age of the Louisiana farmer is fifty-eight. This raises the concern of how and where our food will come from in the future. Fortunately, this statistic mostly applies to row crops such as beans, corn, sugar, rice, and wheat, whereas fruit and vegetable farmers (professional and hobbyist) range widely in age.

Community, home, and school gardens are not a new trend. Like fashion, garden popularity cycles every so many years. Vegetable gardens were initially grown to fill the basic need for food, then trended as a patriotic duty of civilians in World War I and World War II. In the 1960s, "flower children" looking for a more natural lifestyle took up gardening. Today, nature lovers and environmental enthusiasts are among those who regularly garden. With the USDA's focus on reducing childhood obesity by promoting healthy living, it is no wonder that gardeners of every age are all around us. Twenty- and thirty-somethings have developed thriving community gardens throughout Louisiana. From young, hip gardeners in New Iberia growing gorgeous produce in trendy hydroponic towers to parents in their thirties and forties supplementing their income through vegetable production in the southern and central regions of Louisiana, gardening is not a hobby likely to be ditched in lieu of more modern electronic activities.

Slipping into your retirement years? Gardening is still the perfect activity. Just ask any of the fifty-five-and-older crowd who are growing vegetables at their homes. Some retirees are planting in the traditional manner in large gardens with rows pulled up by tractors, while others are growing enough for their families and neighbors in easy-to-access raised beds and containers.

The great thing about a garden is that it can be as large or small as you want it to be. Not all gardens are planted in rows—as long as the container can hold eight inches of soil, you can grow a vegetable plant. Many people garden on their patios in pots or in their zero lot line in narrow raised beds. As long as you have sunlight, you can garden. So relax, this is going to be easy and fun!

Gardening fits in well with so many lifestyles. Those who travel or choose to stay out of the sun in the summertime can simply cover the garden with black cloth to prevent weeds until the weather cools in the fall. For those looking for a year-round hobby, all twelve months of the year can be consumed with cultivating a garden. One of the best reasons to start gardening? Friends! Extra tomatoes, eggplant, watermelon, cabbage, and cucumbers are the perfect conversation starter with people in your community. Following the tips in this book will ensure you are successful.

Conventional and Organic Gardening . . . What's the Difference?

Gardeners have different reasons for growing their own food. For some, it's just a hobby; others enjoy nurturing and watching seeds grow into something they'll eat. Some garden out of necessity, or to obtain food that has a "fresher" taste. Others garden so that they know exactly how their food was produced. No matter the reason why you grow vegetables or how you do it, it is important to understand there are multiple gardening methods.

You have probably heard of conventional and organic gardening and maybe even of sustainable gardening. But what do those terms mean? Below are the most basic definitions of each.

- *Conventional gardening* is growing food with the use of synthetic fertilizers and pesticides.
- *Organic gardening* is growing food using fertilizer and pesticides but only those originating from natural sources. In addition to replacing synthetic fertilizers and pesticides with natural forms, organic gardeners rely heavily on the promotion of soil health by managing natural microorganisms in the soil and encouraging beneficial insects and good agricultural practices such as keeping the garden area clean, using natural mulches, and practicing crop rotation.
- *Sustainable gardening* is growing food with the responsible use of fertilizer and pesticides. Sustainable gardeners establish thresh-

olds for pests (weeds, insects, and disease). Only after this threshold has been exceeded will sustainable gardeners use conventional gardening methods. Sustainable gardeners also use organic sources of fertilizer and pesticides prior to using synthetic sources.

Throughout this book, examples of all three methods will be provided. There is no right or wrong method of gardening . . . just the one that suits you best.

Whether they prefer conventional, organic, or sustainable gardening, good gardeners do not rely solely on quick fixes and pesticides to grow a bountiful garden. All three types of gardeners also follow best management practices (BMPs), including the following techniques:

1. Water at the base of plants to prevent wet foliage and limit fungus and bacteria spread.
2. Plant the correct crops in the correct season.
3. Manage insects using a combination of beneficial insects, traps, and pesticides.
4. Practice good weed control in and out of the garden.
5. Use compost and aged manures as well as fertilizers appropriately.
6. Rotate crops by family.
7. Regularly clean garden tools.
8. Always measure chemicals. **Do not** estimate the amount of pesticide or fertilizer, regardless of source, prior to applying.

Vegetables Are Not Limited to the Backyard

Say the word "garden," and people automatically picture roses in full bloom and lush tropical landscapes. But fruit and vegetable gardens can be just as attractive. If you need a little inspiration to start your own garden, you can find wonderful examples throughout Louisiana.

Houmas House plantation in the community of Darrow touts many beautifully landscaped gardens. One of my favorite spots is the small cottage garden located right outside of the plantation restaurant. Its short picket fence sets the seasonal scene for asparagus, artichokes, greens, and tomatoes.

White Oak plantation in Baton Rouge has many vegetable gardens—some in raised beds, others in short, small rows. Enjoy walking through this vegetable garden and small fig orchard, and take a moment to visit the pigs and chickens also being raised on the grounds of this beautiful home.

Burden Museum and Gardens in Baton Rouge is home to a quarter-acre children's garden where little ones can run, play, and taste anything and everything growing in the garden. The property also has a historical vegetable garden, located at the back of the property outside of the Rural Life Museum.

New Iberia community gardeners allow visitors to tour their hydroponic garden and locals to partake in the garden by starting their own plots.

Tuten Park in Lake Charles has several raised beds maintained by societies, groups, troops, and individuals, growing a mixture of ornamental and vegetable crops. Come to the garden to sit and relax or play at the playground.

In Central and North Louisiana, there are many gardens worth walking through for inspiration. Visit the many community gardens in the Shreveport area organized by local gardeners and the Red River Coalition of Community Gardeners to see how to build raised beds and admire vegetables grown by local residents. Or check out one of the many Good Food Project community and school gardens run by the Food Bank of Central Louisiana in Alexandria. In the appendix to this book, I have listed a number of Louisiana gardens you will enjoy visiting.

Remember the golden rule when visiting community gardens: Those who grow the produce are the ones who reap the harvest. Be courteous of these public spaces. Occasionally, you will come across a bed where a sign is posted notifying visitors that harvesting is okay. In these cases, take some for yourself but leave enough so the next person can have the same experience as you. If signs are not posted, admire the produce from afar.

TOMATOES
CUCUMBERS
YELLOW SQUASH
SWEET ONIONS
ZUCCHINI

CHOOSING THE BEST LOCATION FOR YOUR GARDEN

What vegetables are easiest to grow? How many plants are needed to feed my family? Are rows, raised beds, or containers best? Each gardener will answer these questions somewhat differently as no two gardens are exactly alike. But there are several characteristics that all gardens have in common . . . well, a common thread in successful gardens at least! Be aware of these in selecting the location of your garden:

- Sunlight
- Drainage
- Proximity to a water source
- Visibility from your home

Sunlight

The sun is the ultimate source of food and energy for a plant. It is the catalyst in the process of photosynthesis. Because of the sun's energy, not only does plant growth occur, but all living creatures on earth have food. Just as children require basic nutrition to grow into adults, plants need sunlight to grow and mature into something we would like to eat! Most spring vegetable crops require 6–8 hours of direct sunlight each day to yield quality produce. Spring crops that require the most sunlight are those that form a flower, then produce a fruit. Examples include peppers, tomatoes, eggplant, squash, cucumbers, pumpkins, and watermelon. Fall leafy crops—including cabbage, greens (mustard, turnip, kale, chard), spinach, lettuce, broccoli, and Brussels sprouts—will produce heavy yields with less daily sunlight but still prefer at least 5–7 hours of direct sun.

Look for the most open spot in your yard. Observe how the light changes throughout the day and from season to season. Avoid tree lines and structures such as sheds, garages, and your house that might shade the garden from the morning or afternoon sun. If the only space you have is really shady, try a few mustard greens or leaf lettuce and you just might be successful. If that works . . . keep trying additional leafy crops to see what you can get away with!

Drainage

Vegetables do not like "wet feet." If the roots of vegetable crops are saturated for more than a few days, they will start to rot. Rotting roots reduce or completely stop plant growth. Seeds started in saturated soil are likely to rot before they germinate. Seedlings that emerge from the ground but look as though they've been pinched at the base of the stem are suffering from "damping off," a disease caused by a combination of fungus in the soil, too much water, and usually colder air temperatures. In selecting your garden site, avoid areas that hold water for several days after a rain, such as ditches and low spots. If your yard has very poor drainage, you can still grow vegetables—just improve drainage by adding in drain lines, or simply build a raised bed.

Proximity to a Water Source

On average, most vegetable crops require an inch of water per week. Giving the garden enough water is just as important as providing sunlight. Water is also required for photosynthesis. Unfortunately, there is no magic formula for how much to water because soil types range greatly across Louisiana. Sandy soils drain much faster than clay soils. Frequent irrigation is required to prevent sandy soils from completely drying out, whereas clay soils require deeper and less frequent applications of water. The only way to tell if your garden needs to be watered is by looking at it. As you scout the area for water needs, you might also catch an unwanted insect or two. **Scouting weekly is very important**. Allowing plants to wilt results in both growth delays and reduced yields.

Key times a plant needs water are when it is first planted (the first two weeks after planting) and when it is blooming. Relying on the rain is okay but may seriously affect your yields. Do not rely solely on weather forecasts. Always be prepared to water the garden. Even though Louisiana receives an average of sixty inches of rainfall annually, showers do not occur on a consistent basis. Installing a drip hose with a simple timer or just being close to a water faucet for hand watering is important. Look on the perimeter of your home . . . where is the faucet? If it's on the opposite side of the house from where you intend to plant your garden, you might consider switching sides. Connecting several hoses together each time you need to water isn't feasible—think leaks, heavy hoses, and wet feet . . . what a bad combination on a hot day after a hard day at work.

Visibility from Your Home

This last characteristic is not as important for plant growth as sun, water, and drainage—but it should not be ignored, either. Gardens planted near your home, ones that are walked by on a daily basis, are usually better maintained than those grown far away from the house. You would be surprised by the damage that can be inflicted on your garden in a matter of just a few days by a tomato hornworm, a raccoon, or a heavy rain followed by an outbreak of weeds and grass. There is no point in spending the time required to grow a vegetable garden if squirrels and other critters run away with all your hard work because you haven't checked it in a few days. Make sure *you* are enjoying the bounty of the garden.

Combine the above characteristics when you choose your garden site, and you will set yourself up for success!

GARDEN DESIGN
CONTAINERS, RAISED BEDS, AND IN-GROUND GARDENS

Containers

Vegetable plants can grow quite well in containers. If growing larger plants such as tomatoes, peppers, and eggplant, you'll do better using containers that are at least 5 gallons in size. Five-gallon containers are approximately 11 inches wide and 10 inches deep. Many hardware stores and plant nurseries sell them. Of course, larger containers are also acceptable. Smaller plants with a shallow root system, such as herbs and lettuce, will perform well in 3-gallon pots (10 inches wide and 8.8 inches deep). I tend to favor larger containers because they need less frequent watering. Remember, each time a plant severely wilts, the harvest will decrease. Also, the more often you water, the more likely you are to leach valuable nutrients, leaving your plants with fewer nutrients for proper growth.

Decorative containers add to the beauty of the garden. Simply make sure they are large enough and have been manufactured with drainage holes. If the selected container has no holes, you can add them. Use a drill or nail and hammer to add drainage holes to plastic, wood, and metal containers. Adding drainage to ceramic containers is more difficult. Use a drill with a masonry bit to avoid cracking the container. Bring the pot with you to the local hardware store so they can help you choose the correct bit. Some gardeners also place a piece of tape over the hole location for extra insurance against the pot cracking. Or simply place a cheap plastic pot that already has drainage holes inside the decorative pot.

Tips for Growing Vegetables in Containers

- Drainage is *not* optional.
- Size matters. The larger the container, the less frequently you will need to water it. This reduces your chances of plant wilt.
- For larger-rooted plants (eggplant, tomatoes, cucumbers, squash, etc.), you must choose a 5-gallon container or larger.
- Consider yourself a patio gardener? Then place saucers under containers to prevent soil that leaches from the pot from staining your concrete.
- Looking for a container that holds multiple plants? Consider a hydroponic or aeroponic tower. Many online companies sell these as kits, with average prices ranging from $100 to $500. The towers hold 5–20 plants and generally take up five feet of space. This is a great option for space-limited gardeners, but read the directions carefully. These take some patience and practice before you will master growing plants in them.
- Planting in extremely large containers? Invest in plant stands with wheels. These will greatly reduce the risk of hurting your back when shifting containers on the patio. After you add soil, the containers will be *very* heavy.
- Between seasons or before planting a new crop, mix the soil in the container from the top to the bottom. This is especially important in large pots, where air and water pockets form over time.
- Consider investing in a moisture meter. These inexpensive meters provide an easy-to-read measure of the amount of water in the container that correlates with commands such as "Water Now," "Water Acceptable," "Wait to Water Later," or "This Pot is Saturated . . . Do Something!"

Raised Beds

Raised beds can be constructed in all shapes, sizes, lengths, and widths. Practically speaking, the width of a raised bed should not exceed what you can comfortably reach to the middle of without stepping in the bed. Each time you step into a raised bed, you compact the soil. The main reason to build raised beds is to avoid having to till the soil with heavy equipment between seasons. Consider constructing the beds only twice as wide as your arm length. On the same note, raised beds can be any depth as long as they hold at least 8 inches of soil. Make the structure a little deeper than 8 inches so that you can add a mulch layer on top of the soil and not have it or the soil float out of the bed when watering plants.

When I am constructing beds, the minimum depth I use is 12 inches: 8 inches for soil, 2 inches for mulch materials, and another 2 inches of lip space. If bending over gives you trouble, build the bed 2 to 4 feet high. The taller the bed, the more soil is needed to fill it. Soil can be expensive, ranging $20–$50 per yard for a good garden mix, so be prepared to stomach a little extra cost with taller beds.

Common Materials for Building Raised Beds

- Treated lumber. Treated lumber manufactured after 2003 for residential areas no longer contains arsenic.
- Nontreated wood products that can withstand Louisiana's wet weather for a limited time. These include cedar, mahogany (very expensive), white oak, teak, and black walnut. You should still limit contact with the ground as much as possible. Consider a single layer of bricks under these beds or a layer of weed barrier or shade cloth for added protection.
- Plastic lumber composites. These can be purchased through many online garden stores in sizes cut for particular-shaped raised beds. Note that these can be very expensive.
- Cinder blocks.
- Bricks.
- Pavers.
- Old railroad ties. These work wonderfully, but be sure to plant veggies at least one foot away from the edge of the bed if the creosote is fresh. The creosote may burn the tips of roots and cause a stunting of the plant. *Note:* Use extreme caution if cutting railroad ties as the creosote can cause chemical burns to your skin.
- Pine straw, wheat straw, and other square hay bales. These can be arranged in any shape. The center of the shape is then filled with soil and planted exactly like a raised bed.

- Large, round hay bales. Simply scoop out a shovelful of hay in multiple areas. Fill the voids with compost or soil, and plant. Think of this raised bed as a large strawberry pot.

Raised-Bed Ground Preparation

Before or immediately after constructing the raised bed, remove any grass and weeds directly below and around the site to prevent them from encroaching in the garden space. This can be accomplished in several ways.

- *Conventional manner:* Use a nonselective systemic herbicide to kill all weeds. "Nonselective" means the herbicide will kill both grasses (narrow foliage plants) and broadleaf weeds. "Systemic" means it moves from the foliage of the plant into the root, killing the entire unwanted plant. Always follow all directions on the herbicides label. **Do not over- or underapply the rate.** Changing the rate can result in 1) the weeds not being killed; 2) the product polluting the environment; and/or 3) damaging the vegetable plants you intend to plant at a later date. Once the herbicide has been applied and the plants start to die, you can simply remove the weeds and grass and fill the garden bed with fresh soil.
- *Organic manner:* Place black plastic, cardboard, or dark cloth over the grass and weeds to block sunlight and kill the vegetation. This will take up to four weeks for a complete kill and works best when grass and weeds are not dormant. Then dig up the weeds and roots and fill the site with garden soil. Because a systemic herbicide was not used, the roots of perennial weeds such as bermudagrass will still be viable and will regrow after this process. Root removal is crucial. Do not leave the plastic at the bottom of the bed. This can cause drainage issues. If you really want a layer of protection between the ground and the trucked-in soil, cut slits in the plastic layer or use a water-permeable cloth.
- *Organic manner:* Use a cultivator such as a string trimmer to physically remove all tops of grass and weeds and then dig into the soil at least two inches with the cultivator to turn the roots. Rake out all plant matter (tops and roots), build the bed, and fill with soil.

In-Ground Gardens

In-ground gardens can be small with a few very short rows or very large, encompassing up to an acre. Advantages of gardening directly in the ground include plenty of space for root growth, and that the native soil adds to the "taste" of the vegetables produced. This is sometimes referred to as *terroir,* or the interaction of the soil, topography, and climate along with plant genetics to form a particular taste. Wine and champagne enthusiasts often use this word to explain why certain beverages have a unique flavor. *Terroir* is not limited to regions of France; even here in Louisiana we have *terroir.* For many years and even today, growers in Plaquemines Parish have referred to their homegrown tomatoes as "Creole" tomatoes, claiming the soil gave them that much sought-after flavor. "Creole" is now a marketing term used by growers across the state to describe Louisiana-grown tomatoes.

One disadvantage of in-ground gardens is that weeds tend to creep into these gardens faster than in raised beds and containers. But when managed for weeds, in-ground gardens have an impressive look. Generally, tilling the soil and making the rows is more easily accomplished with equipment and not by hand. If you intend to grow a large in-ground garden, assume you will invest major sweat equity. How to prepare the soil for your in-ground garden is covered in the next chapter.

SOIL MATTERS, FEED IT

What Is Soil and Why Is It So Important?

Soil is the uppermost portion of the earth's crust. It is usually composed of decaying organic matter such as leaves and sticks combined with living creatures such as worms, bacteria, and fungi, and bits of rock. However, all soils are not created equal. Soil types throughout Louisiana can vary greatly in color, texture, and chemistry. And that's if you're looking at the ground! Bagged soil and potting mixes referred to as "media" are also vastly different. Soilless media are made of peat moss, bark, vermiculite, perlite, sand, and sometimes compost. Regardless of what soil type you garden in, testing it every three years is important. A routine soil test submitted to an independent lab or to the LSU AgCenter's Soil Testing and Plant Analysis Lab will tell you your soil's pH and levels of macro- and micronutrients needed for plant growth. When you receive your results, amend the soil or medium accordingly.

Taking Soil Samples and Understanding the Results

When taking soil samples, don't sample from only one area in the garden space. Take multiple shovels of soil from several areas within the space you intend to develop into a garden. Mix all of the samples together, then submit a subsample from the entire garden area. Most labs only need a pint of soil. There is no need to mail in an entire bucketful.

When filling out your forms, be sure to write what vegetables you intend to plant. Otherwise, the lab won't be able to tell you how to amend the soil properly.

Your test results will include the pH level of your soil. pH is an extremely important factor in determining if soil nutrients will be available to the plants. A pH between 5.5 and 7 is ideal for most vegetable crops. Potatoes and strawberries prefer a little more acidic soil, while other crops like basic soil (near 7 on a scale of 0–14).

Test results will also include levels of nitrogen (N), phosphorus (P), and potassium (K), the three macro or main elements a plant needs to grow. Memorizing ideal levels of each of these nutrients is not necessary as most soil labs will specify if you are low, average, or high in these macronutrients. The same holds true with the micronutrients, such as calcium, boron, magnesium, manganese, iron, and sulfur.

Choosing the Best Soil or Medium for Containers and Raised Beds

When selecting soil for containers and raised beds, be aware that as of this writing there is only one commercially bagged medium available specifically for use for vegetable crops grown in raised beds. Many bagged media products have a picture of vegetables on the bag and claim they can be used in container and raised-bed gardening. Read the directions carefully because these mixes often state that you must mix the contents of the bag with an equal amount of native garden soil before adding it to the container or bed. This is because bagged media are typically heavy in peat. Peat moss holds an enormous amount of water. Vegetable crops should be grown in moist but not saturated soils. These are not my preferred types of media, simply because you can encounter problems when growing in native soils. Native soil has good but also bad bacteria.

If possible, find a local nursery that prepares media. Look for a medium that is roughly one-third peat moss, one-third bark, and one-third sand. The bark used in media for vegetable production should be well composted. Large pieces of bark take a long time to decompose. While they are decomposing, they physically bind with nutrients in the soil, limiting nutrient availability to plants. Plants may appear sick as a result, even though the soil has plenty of macro- and micronutrients in it.

Ask the manager to see a soil test for the medium. The pH should be between 5.5 and 7. Also ask if any fertilizer was added. Very often, bagged and specialty mixed media will have fertilizer incorporated into them. If this is the case, there is no need to "preplant fertilize." You will see preplant fertilizer referred to in chapter 6 for each vegetable crop. Preplant fertilizing generally occurs 1–3 weeks prior to planting the crop. A medium with fertilizer incorporated in it has already been preplant fertilized.

Adding the Medium to Containers

Make sure the container has good drainage. Fill the container with an appropriate depth of medium, leaving a 3-inch lip. A common question is, if my container is large, do I have to fill it completely with soil/medium? Answer: No. Some gardeners place pebbles, old crawfish bags, or packing peanuts at the bottom of the container. This is okay as long as you still have suitable depth of medium for the vegetable or herb you want to plant.

Place 1–2 inches of mulch materials on top of the medium for weed prevention. Leave a 1-inch lip so the water and mulch materials do not run over the sides of the container when you water in your plants.

Adding the Medium to Raised Beds

Soil for raised beds can be native soil, bagged media, or a combination of both. After you have removed existing weeds and vegetation from the raised-bed area (as described in the previous chapter), you are ready to add the soil. Fill the raised bed with soil until it is almost full, leaving a 4-inch lip. You should add at least 8 inches of medium to any bed in which the native soil was not tilled. If you removed weeds and then tilled the native soil, adding an additional 8 inches of medium on top is not necessary—but also not harmful, as raised beds can be as tall as you like. Apply a 1–3 inch layer of mulch, using materials such as pine needles, leaves, hay, or shredded newspaper. Remember, no heavy fresh bark. Make sure you leave space for a 1-inch lip so that the medium and mulch do not run over the side of the raised bed after you plant and water it in.

Preparing Soil for In-Ground Gardening

Prior to tilling the soil, use any of the methods of weed removal discussed in the previous chapter, under "Raised-Bed Ground Preparation." After you have removed the weeds and existing vegetation, it is time to till the soil. If your soil type has clay in it, you will need to build the rows up. Clay soils tend to hold more water than sandy soils, so after heavy rains your plants' roots may rot. Form rows at least 6 inches high.

To form rows (without a tractor), simply:

1. Till the ground to a depth of at least 6 inches.
2. Using a shovel, scoop soil from what will become your walkway and throw it in toward the middle of the row. Continue this process until you've built up one side of the row and then repeat the process on the other side. This may have to be repeated several times before the row is formed.
3. Use a hard rake to knock down the tops of the rows, forming a flat surface. Rows, measuring from one walkway to the next, should not be less than 24 inches wide.
4. Fill in the walkways with mulch, preferably pine straw, hay, or leaves. Using fresh woody mulch materials may render valuable nutrients unavailable as they decompose in the soil. The mulch layer between rows should be at least 4 inches thick to control weed seed germination.

If you have extremely sandy soil, building rows is not as critical as when the soil is heavy in clay. In fact, if your soil is mostly sandy, it is best to grow on flat ground so that rows do not dry out too quickly before the next rain or irrigation. Sand particles are larger than clay particles, so they do not fit as tightly together and thus allow water to drain more quickly than clay. In sandy soils, a gardener should water more frequently and less deeply than if growing in clay soils.

Fertilizing the Garden

Proper nutrition is important for proper plant growth. Check out the quick guide below to determine if you have a macronutrient deficiency problem. This is only a guide. Submitting foliage samples to a registered plant lab will inform you of what nutrients your plants may be lacking. When selecting a sample, take a portion of the foliage that is showing symptoms but also combine it with foliage from the middle of the plant, not the very new or very old leaves.

Macro Elements

Element	Role in Plant Development	Symptoms If Plant Is Deficient
Nitrogen	Helps build vegetative growth. A building block for proteins and amino acids and the primary component of chlorophyll.	Older or lower leaves are yellow. Plant size is stunted.
Phosphorus	Helps plants develop roots and aids in flowering and seed development.	Purple to dark green foliage, especially on older, lower leaves. Fruiting is slow to occur.
Potassium	Helps build plant enzymes and is used in photosynthesis. Is thought to play a critical role in helping plants survive drought, cold, and pest stress.	Older leaves look burned along the margins. Noticeable uneven ripening of fruit.

Notice Something Strange about the Foliage?

Youngest leaves/upper foliage is displaying symptoms:

- *Manganese deficiency*—New foliage has yellow spots, and eventually the entire leaf will turn yellow. Sometimes foliage will have holes in it.
- *Iron deficiency*—New foliage is white or very pale yellow with green veins.
- *Sulfur deficiency*—New foliage is very pale, and often the entire plant will turn a very pale shade of green soon afterwards. Sulfur deficiency is not very common in Louisiana.
- *Calcium deficiency*—New foliage is stunted and distorted.
- *Boron deficiency*—New foliage is distorted in shape. Many vegetables in the Brassica family will have hollow stems.
- *Copper deficiency*—Tips of younger leaves turn yellow.

Middle foliage is displaying symptoms:

- *Zinc deficiency*—Middle foliage is very pale yellow, often white in color.

Oldest leaves/bottom foliage is displaying symptoms:

- *Magnesium deficiency*—Lower and middle foliage is yellow with dark veins. Generally, the leaves yellow from the outside moving inward.
- *Molybdenum deficiency*—Older foliage turns yellow, usually from outside inward. Plants will become stunted and edges of leaves distorted. This is most commonly a problem in acidic soils (pH lower than 7).

There are two key times to fertilize a vegetable garden, often referred to as preplant fertilizer application and side-dress fertilizer application.

Preplant Fertilizer. In raised beds and in-ground gardens, apply preplant fertilizer to the soil 1 to 3 weeks before planting seeds or transplants and right after soil preparation. The 1–3 week period is to ensure the garden area receives rain or has been irrigated prior to planting. Generally, a complete fertilizer (one that has equal amounts of N-P-K) is used. Common examples include 13-13-13 or 8-8-8. You can either broadcast the fertilizer over the entire garden or raised bed before establishing rows, or you can form rows or designated planting areas in a raised bed and then band the fertilizer down the center of that planting area. The "band" is a straight line of fertilizer applied deep enough in the soil so that the roots of a new seedling or transplant or a seed sown into the garden does not come in direct contact with the fertilizer. Rather, the plant should be allowed to grow for a week or more before it touches the band of fertilizer. The band is usually placed down the center of the row, directly beneath where you will plant the crop, 4–5 inches below the soil surface.

In container gardening, preplant fertilizer application depends on the type of medium used. Most bagged media come "charged," or with fertilizer already added. The first time you use such a mix, preplant fertilizer is not necessary. If the same soil remains in the container over several years, add compost or a few tablespoons of fertilizer as a preplant application. Always water the container after fertilizing and wait a week to plant.

Side-Dressing. Side-dressing is applying fertilizer to vegetable crops after they have started to grow. Side-dress fruiting crops (ones that produce a flower and then a fruit) at first bloom set and repeat if desired at second or third bloom set. Side-dress leafy vegetable crops two to three weeks after seeding or transplanting. Fertilizers used for side-dressing are often high in nitrogen and low in phosphorus and potassium. This means that the fertilizer bag will have a #-0-0 such as 15-0-0 on the label. Common examples include calcium nitrate ($CaNO_3$), potassium nitrate (KNO_3), and aluminum sulfate, $Al_2\ (SO_4)_3$. Side-dressing is termed such because the fertilizer is applied along the side of the row or to the edge of the raised bed approximately 8 inches from the base of the plant.

In a container, there is often not room to apply a side-dress application 8 inches from the base of the plant. Calcium nitrate and potassium nitrate can still be used, but apply no more than 1/2 to 1 teaspoon per plant in the container at any one time. Miracle-Gro and other trade-name fertilizers that have *soluble fertilizer* can also be applied at low rates (read the label and use recommended rates) as a side-dress application. Avoid over-application of fertilizer in containers as salts in the soil can easily build up if watered infrequently or inconsistently.

Common Fertilizers

Prior to fertilizing your garden, have a soil test conducted at least every three years. This will tell you how much fertilizer to apply. There is no reason to apply additional nutrients if soil levels are already high. It is important to note that many soils in Louisiana are naturally high in phosphorus and potassium as these nutrients do not leach as readily through the soil profile as others. Nitrogen easily evaporates into the atmosphere, leaving soils more often depleted of this valuable nutrient. The three numbers on a bag of fertilizer represent percentages of N-P-K. Micronutrients will also appear on the label if they are contained in the fertilizer.

Individual gardeners should decide what kinds of fertilizer they are willing to use. The examples given in the paragraphs above are all synthetic options. Other common fertilizers used in vegetable gardens include:

- 8-24-24
- 10-10-10

- 5-10-5
- Urea
- Ammonium sulfate (not great for brassica crops; makes them extra smelly when cooking)
- Nitrate of soda (organically labeled but only for up to 20% of the crop's needs)
- Cottonseed meal (organically labeled)
- Bonemeal (organically labeled)
- Worm teas and castings (organically labeled)
- Compost
- Manures
- Miracle-Gro, Schultz, Peters, and other trade-name liquid fertilizers

Fertilizer Tips

- Okra, beans, and peas rarely need side-dress applications of fertilizer. Only do so if they appear deficient in nutrients. Over-fertilizing these crops will prevent bloom and thus prevent fruit and pod development.
- **Always** water after applying fertilizer. Otherwise, you risk burning a plant's roots.
- Apply fertilizer to the soil, not to plant foliage, unless you are applying specific micronutrients. The majority of N, P, and K enters a plant through its roots.
- If you are gardening in containers, check the potting soil you purchase. Most already contain sufficient levels of preplant fertilizer. If fertilizer is in the mix, adding more may actually hurt the plant.
- Side-dress fertilizer applications should be placed approximately 6–8 inches from the base of the plant to avoid burning it.
- Manures should always be aged, meaning they have been composted for at least 6–12 months before entering the garden. Fresh manures are very "hot"—high in nitrogen—and can potentially contain microorganisms harmful for both plant and human health.
- Never use manures as a side-dress application of fertilizer.

In the vegetable listings in chapter 5, recommended rates of fertilizer are given in terms of low, medium, and heavy. Read the label on the bag of fertilizer you select to determine what amounts low, medium, and heavy represent. Every fertilizer is slightly different. Therefore, reading and adhering to the label is very important.

Below is an example of varying rates using 13-13-13 synthetic fertilizer.

- *Low fertilizer rate:* 0.3 to 0.5 lbs. (about 1 cup) of 13-13-13 for every 10 feet in a raised bed or in-ground garden row.
- *Medium fertilizer rate:* 0.6 to 0.8 lbs (about 1.5 cups) of 13-13-13 for every 10 feet in a raised bed or in-ground garden.
- *Heavy fertilizer rate:* 0.9 to 1.5 lbs. (about 2–3 cups) of 13-13-13 for every 10 feet in a raised bed or in-ground garden.

Assume 10 feet in length represents a row 2–4 feet wide, so these rates are appropriate for 20–40 square feet of garden space. Because gardens are formed in various sizes and shapes, appropriate amounts of fertilizer must be calculated to the specific garden in which you grow.

If using a soilless medium, check to see if fertilizer is already included. There is no need to apply preplant fertilizer to crops grown in a container using a soilless medium.

Remember, more is not always better. It is one thing to lose a plant because of weather and another thing to burn the plant thinking a little more fertilizer might boost growth.

MANAGING THE GARDEN AREA
INSECTS, DISEASE, VIRUSES, AND WEEDS

Insect Management

How do I control insects that are ruining my vegetable garden? Always wait to see the insect first or at least inspect the damage it caused before applying a pesticide. Many times, a plant specialist can identify the type of insect just by viewing the damage it left behind. Do not spray preventative insecticides—you do not want to accidentally kill a beneficial insect or apply an insecticide so early that it is ineffective when the actual critters find their way to the garden.

The Good and the Bad

There are beneficial insects as well as pests. Beneficial insects may eat the "bad bugs" (pests) or help pollinate the crop. A few examples of beneficial insects include bees, assassin bugs, lacewings, and—probably the most well known—ladybugs (scientifically referred to as lady beetles). Pests include aphids, thrips, mites, stinkbugs, leaf-footed bugs, worms and loopers, caterpillars, snails and slugs, cucumber beetles and more. Pests are bad for the garden not simply because they eat the produce we want; often they transmit viruses and disease to our plants by harboring bacteria and fungus in their mouthparts. Each time they feed on the plants, they have the opportunity to spread more problems.

Identifying the insect is necessary to determine whether it is good or bad. You must also be able to recognize the insect in all stages of its life cycle. Unlike humans, juvenile insects do not always look like smaller versions of adults. Insects go through complete or incomplete metamorphosis. In incomplete metamorphosis, the juvenile insect looks almost identical to the adult but is smaller in size. A good example is the grasshopper; as it molts or grows, it simply gets bigger and may change shades of color. By contrast, insects that undergo complete metamorphosis look completely different in each stage of the life cycle. One insect that undergoes complete metamorphosis is the ladybug. In a simplified way of looking at a ladybug's life cycle, it undergoes four major stages: egg, larva, pupa, and adult. Many people want to kill ladybugs during the larva stage because they appear ferocious and are many in number and we are sure they are damaging our plants. But they are not; ladybugs feed on soft-bodied insects like aphids and should be left alone in the garden.

So, how do you gain all this identification knowledge so that you know which insects to suppress and which to let freely move through the space? Scout your garden often! Turn over the foliage because no matter good or bad, most insects hang out on the undersides of leaves. If you find something, take a photo of it. You can email the photo or bring it in to your local LSU AgCenter county agent for identification. Samples may also be brought to local plant nursery professionals or to an exterminator who routinely visits your home. Don't have a camera? Catch the insect in a jar! Just make sure to bring it in relatively fresh. I was once given a spider with only three legs left to identify.

Instead of spraying immediately the first time you see a pest, define a threshold at which you feel comfortable allowing this insect to be in your garden. My thresholds change depending on the insect and the damage it is causing. Once that threshold is crossed, it is time to spray, set traps, or release beneficial insects. Having a hard time defining a threshold? Ask your LSU AgCenter county agent about the insect. Does it vector a disease or virus? Does the insect eat the portion of the plant you want, or other portions? Also keep a close eye on the plant. How bad is the damage in a few days? If half the plant is gone in a couple of days, the threshold may be one insect. If the damage is hardly noticeable, the threshold will be set much higher. See the table below for general control methods. Of course, these control methods are not inclusive; new chemistries are constantly being developed for garden use. If you use a technique or chemical that is not listed, first read the label. You are eating these plants and are most likely growing them because you want to know they were grown in an environmentally sound and safe manner for you and your family to consume. The label should state the insect that is the problem, the exact crops you intend to spray it on, and the number of days you need to wait from spraying to harvesting (PHI or pre-harvest interval). Adhere to the label and the rate on the label and you will be just fine!

Remember, the better you care for your plants (applying appropriate amounts of water and fertilizer), the stronger and healthier they will be and the better the chances they will overcome damage from pests. Just as a healthy person can often fight off a common cold, so can a healthy plant often fight off pests. On the other hand, weak, forgotten, neglected plants are extremely susceptible to insects, disease, and virus.

Below is a list of the top 10 "bad" insects that show up annually in Louisiana vegetable gardens. Of course there are others, but these are of most concern to beginning gardeners.

Top 10 Bad Insects

<table>
<tr><th>Common Name</th><th colspan="2">Common Control Methods</th></tr>
<tr><td></td><td>Organic</td><td>Synthetic*</td></tr>
<tr><td>Worms</td><td>Hand pick or spray Bt
(Bacillus thuringiensis), a naturally occurring bacterium.</td><td>Apply carbaryl, spinosad, pyrethroids, or bifenthrin products.</td></tr>
<tr><td>Loopers</td><td>Hand pick or spray Bt.</td><td>Apply carbaryl, spinosad, pyrethroids, or bifenthrin products.</td></tr>
<tr><td>Leaf-footed bugs</td><td rowspan="2">Plant a trap crop of sunflowers near the garden. Spray the trap crop more and your edible crop less to reduce overall populations. Hand pick or vacuum these insects off plants.</td><td rowspan="2">Apply carbaryl or bifenthrin products.</td></tr>
<tr><td>Stinkbugs</td></tr>
<tr><td>Aphids</td><td>Use insecticidal soaps, horticultural oils, or purchase ladybugs.</td><td>Apply bifenthrin, imidacloprid, or malathion** products.</td></tr>
<tr><td>Flea beetles</td><td>If only attacking foliage of plants that are not harvested for foliage (i.e. tomatoes, eggplant), do not treat the plant. Before the pest arrives, use row covers. Or place yellow sticky traps throughout the garden.</td><td>Apply carbaryl, bifenthrin, or malathion products.</td></tr>
</table>

Common Name	Common Control Methods	
	Organic	Synthetic*
Vine borers	Wrap base of seedling stems with foil, making sure that the foil is both above and below the soil line when planted. Row covers can be used from planting until flowering. Once flowers appear, remove covers so that the crop can be pollinated.	Apply carbaryl, bifenthrin, or pyrethroid products.
Cucumber beetles	Deep-till after a particularly bad cucumber beetle season, to bury or kill any eggs that might later hatch in the soil. Row covers can be effective if you know this pest visits the garden annually. But put these out early.	Apply carbaryl, bifenthrin, pyrethroids, malathion, or imidacloprid products.
Snails/slugs	Apply diatomaceous earth to the soil around plants, or place shallow saucers of beer even with the soil line. Place a board on the ground in contact with the soil. Daily scrape snails off bottom of board directly into a trash can. Water the base of the plants at night to encourage snails to come out of the soil, and hand pick at night. Remove mulches from directly underneath plants.	Apply products with the active ingredient metaldehyde or iron phosphate baits.
Thrips	Use silver-colored plastic mulch or extra-wide aluminum foil to line the tops of your bed or rows around tomatoes and peppers only. The sunlight reflecting off the mulch or foil prevents insects from seeing the plants so they don't land in your garden. Works best when used on three or more rows side by side.	Apply imidachloprid products.
Whiteflies	Place sticky tape or traps on garden trellises. Encourage beneficial insects such as lacewings; apply horticultural soaps and oils; hand remove; use silver-colored mulch or wide aluminum foil for tomatoes and peppers (see under "Thrips").	Conventional insecticides are not effective in controlling large populations. Try to space plants properly and remove any plants that are extremely infested.

*Not all chemicals are labeled for every vegetable crop. Read the label and make sure the name of the vegetable you are spraying is listed on the label.

**Malathion does not work on all species of aphids. In fact, some aphids are only temporarily bothered by malathion and spraying it encourages them to reproduce at a more rapid than normal rate, building populations rather than reducing them.

Note: There are many different species of each pest mentioned. These insects are not listed in a particular order. Certain pests will be more attracted to particular vegetables than others.

Disease and Virus Management

Disease and viruses are often inevitable in both small and large home gardens. In smaller gardens, preventative measures can greatly reduce the chance of being overwhelmed by disease and virus. Take the following steps to minimize exposure:

- Use proper spacing. Crowded vegetable plants are an open invitation to insects to move into the garden. Insects can spread disease and viruses. Additionally, mold, fungus, and bacterial spores are more likely to spread from one plant onto another during rain events if plants are crowded.
- Apply mulch to the garden area. Mulches help prevent soil from splashing onto the base of plants. Many garden pests are soil borne, so if you can keep soil from splashing onto a plant, especially one that has an injury or an opening, you are more likely to prevent entry of the unwanted organism into the plant.
- Water at the base of the plant. Plants drink through their roots. Very little water enters a plant through its stomata (tiny pores on a leaf surface used mostly to regulate internal plant temperature). Water running over leaf surfaces moves unwanted spores from one plant onto another. Using drip irrigation is a great choice for both irrigation and disease prevention.
- If using overhead irrigation, water in the morning, to allow plant foliage to dry before evening.
- Avoid buying transplants that have disease or virus symptoms or that are covered in insects. It is worth paying a little extra or making two or three stops to find healthy plants in order not to bring new problems into your garden.
- If you save seed from your vegetable plants, avoid saving seed from any crop that was heavily affected by a virus. Viruses can sometimes be carried over in the seed from one season to the next. Just start fresh.
- Remove weeds from the garden. Weeds harbor insects, and insects harbor disease and viruses.
- Plant a variety of vegetable crops. Limiting your garden to one or two crops (monoculture) oftentimes makes it more difficult to control disease. Rotate crop families between seasons. We will discuss crop rotation in the next chapter.

Controlling Weeds in Backyard Gardens

In containers and raised beds, hand pulling weeds is the best option, unless the situation is out of control and weeds have taken over the garden bed. To prevent weed encroachment:

- Mow grass around gardens, beds, and containers.
- Apply mulch around the vegetable plants, between rows, on top of raised beds, and in containers.
- Pull weeds as soon as you see them. Once they go to seed, it is difficult to manage weeds in later years.

If weeds have already taken over the garden container or raised bed:

- Remove soil from small containers and start over. After a weed has gone to seed, it can leave thousands of seeds in the soil that can germinate for years to come. Replace with fresh soil and plant again.
- In larger raised beds and gardens, remove all vegetable crops after the season is finished and hand pull what weeds you can and till in the rest. Allow weed seeds to re-emerge and immediately spray with an organic or synthetic herbicide. Wait the appropriate amount of time (listed on the label) and then plant your vegetable crops again, hand pulling as weeds emerge.

Weed barriers such as weed cloth, plastic mulches, and groundcover cloth can also be used on a garden's surface to help prevent sunlight from reaching the weed seed. Just be sure to install irrigation underneath if the material is not water permeable (plastic mulches only).

There are three main categories of weeds: grasses (monocots), broadleaf weeds (dicots), and sedges (look like grasses but the stem is triangular). Very few herbicides are labeled for use in a home garden.

Grasses

- *Organic method:* Mix a solution of 50% white vinegar with 50% water and spray on newly emerged grasses. Grasses over 2 inches in height will not be greatly affected by this option. Do not spray this solution on vegetable plants. Before grasses emerge, use herbicides with the active ingredient corn gluten meal. This prevents weed seeds from germinating. *Note:* Many grasses move into gardens through vegetative propagation (e.g., grass clippings with a node or two flying into the garden from lawnmowers, or grass sending out rhizomes/stolons underneath garden beds only to emerge between vegetable plants). Preemergent herbicides are only effective against seeds, not grasses that enter a garden through vegetative propagation.

- *Synthetic method:* After grasses have emerged, use herbicides with the active ingredient sethoxydim. This herbicide can come into contact with broadleaf plants without injuring them. Before grasses emerge, use herbicides with the active ingredient trifluralin (Treflan). *Note:* This chemical is not labeled for use in asparagus, garlic, lettuce, onions, or when any of the cucurbits (squash, cucumbers, melons, pumpkins) are direct seeded into a garden.

Broadleaf Weeds

- *Organic method:* Before broadleaf weeds emerge, use herbicides with the active ingredient corn gluten meal. This prevents weed seeds from germinating.
- *Synthetic method:* Before broadleaf weeds emerge, use herbicides with the active ingredient trifluralin (Treflan). *Note:* This chemical is not labeled for use in asparagus, garlic, lettuce, onions, or when any of the cucurbits (squash, cucumbers, melons, pumpkins) are direct seeded into a garden.

Sedges

- *Organic method:* Fix drainage and irrigation problems in the vegetable garden. Sedges thrive in moist areas. Use a pitchfork to gently pull up soil from under the sedges, then hand remove all underground tubers. Simply pulling the sedge by hand and not removing underground roots only spreads the problem. Apply products with the active ingredient pelargonic acid before the populations rise.
- *Synthetic method:* Use herbicides with the active ingredient glyphosate. They may be sprayed on the sedge, but a more effective

> application is the wipe method. Mix the herbicide in a bucket as recommended on the label. Next, put on a plastic glove and then a cotton glove over the top of your hand. Dip the gloved hand into the bucket of herbicide. With the gloved hand, wipe the sedge blades to ensure sufficient contact of the herbicide to the sedge. You may also do this with a mop or broom. Allow two weeks to pass before pulling the sedge to provide sufficient time for the herbicide to translocate through the plant and kill the roots. *Do not* apply glyphosate products when vegetable crops are in the garden. This should only be done between seasons.

If you do not need immediate results, wait until the season is over or you have finished harvesting and then synthetically control all weeds by spraying herbicides with the active ingredient glyphosate over the entire garden area. Wait two weeks for the herbicide to translocate throughout the plants, then till in or remove the weeds, re-till the soil, and plant again. Wait at least two weeks after spraying any products with the active ingredient glyphosate before planting vegetable crops.

If you are looking for a more sustainable or organic weed-control approach, try solarization to reduce weed seed populations. First, remove all weeds and grasses from the garden area by hand pulling or tilling. Then wet the garden area until it is saturated. Complete saturation is absolutely necessary for this to work. Next, cover the entire garden area with a clear plastic barrier. Clear plastics can be purchased at most hardware stores in large sheets for larger gardens. Using a shovel, bury the edge of the plastic all around the perimeter of the garden area. The sunlight will penetrate the plastic, allowing weed seed to germinate, but the excessive moisture and heat under the plastic will burn the plants. Leaving the plastic on the garden area for 1–3 months during the hottest time of the year (June through September) will greatly reduce weed seed populations as well as reduce some pesky microorganisms. After removing the plastic, lightly till the soil (no more than 3 inches deep), form rows if needed—but try not to disturb the soil below the top 4–6 inches because solarization is usually most effective in the top layer of soil—and plant vegetable crops again. This method can be used for weed control in containers as well.

Weed-Control Tips

- Read the label! Both the vegetable plant and the weed you are trying to control should be listed.
- Do not apply more or less than what is recommended.
- If the label says to wear long sleeves or pants, do so. Some herbicides (even those organically labeled) contain irritants that can cause a rash on your skin.
- Wear closed-toe shoes.
- Avoid spraying herbicides on windy days to prevent drift onto landscape plants.
- After mixing herbicides with water, use immediately. Many break down quickly and will not be as effective in a day or two.
- *Do not* direct seed vegetable crops after applying a pre-emergent herbicide (one that works prior to the weed seed germinating) unless the label states it is okay for that specific crop. These herbicides are effective because they prevent weed seeds from emerging.

BASIC GARDENING TECHNIQUES

Direct Seeding Versus Transplanting

How do I know if I should put seed directly into the ground or plant small seedlings? This is an easy question to answer. If the vegetable is a root crop, always direct seed. Direct seeding beets, carrots, potatoes, turnips, and other root crops enables the plants to grow to their full potential.

Leafy crops, including mustard greens, collard greens, turnip greens, kale, spinach, and leaf lettuces, are also easily planted by directly placing the seed into the ground. Plus, the seed cost of these crops is relatively inexpensive, whereas purchasing seedlings can be cost prohibitive for the gardener on a budget. For example, as of this writing, a 6-pack container of mustard green seedlings costs around $2.00 while a package of mustard seeds (generally 100–500 seeds) costs on average $0.99 to $1.89.

Cheap seeds also extend to beans and peas. These crops generally have excellent germination rates, and because most gardeners want to plant more than ten or so of these plants, seeding is a great way to go.

Cucurbits . . . A fancy term (the family name) for cucumbers, melons, pumpkins, and squash. Members of this family usually perform best when direct seeded. Yes, transplants can be used, but if the roots have started to wrap in the containers, these crops will produce less than those directly seeded into the garden. Be cautious when purchasing transplants of cucurbits.

So, if direct seeding is so inexpensive and easy, then why would a person choose to start with seedlings? Seedlings or transplants offer a gardener many benefits.

- Seed for some plants—tomatoes, peppers, cole crops (that is, cruciferous vegetables), and eggplant, for example—is expensive and hard to germinate. It is just easier on a backyard gardener to purchase, plant, and have immediate success.
- Planting transplants provides you with a head start on harvesting warm-season crops versus those that were direct seeded. On average, you might produce tomatoes 6–10 weeks prior to gardeners who direct seed.
- A transplanted garden shows instant progress for those who want visible results or who have little patience for germination to occur.
- If you grow your own transplants, you choose the varieties you want and don't have to settle for those available locally.

Successional Planting for Small Gardeners

Successional planting is staggering a planting of one vegetable crop over a period of time so that the produce matures gradually and not all at once. Let's say that your garden is made up of 6 rows that are each 50 feet long. If you were to plant one row with cabbage transplants on September 15, you would harvest nearly 120–150 cabbage plants, all within 1–2 weeks. Most families cannot consume or even give away that much cabbage in that short time period. A good alternative would be to use successional planting to space out the harvest period of your cabbage crop. In other words, you would plant the first third of the row on September 15, the second third on October 1, and the third portion of the row on October 15. All three planting dates are acceptable for planting cool-season crops, and now, your family and friends will enjoy fresh cabbage throughout the season using the same amount of space. Successional plantings are generally used for crops that mature all at one time, such as head lettuce, cabbage, cauliflower, potatoes, and others that you harvest only once. Vegetable crops like tomatoes, squash, and cucumbers also tend to produce heavily in a quick period but naturally produce over a month or more, so successional planting is not as important for these crops in smaller gardens.

Planting Crops in Season

Remember that no matter how much attention you give to the garden, if you plant a crop out of season it is likely to fail. Gardeners refer to crops by the season in which they are planted, not always harvested:

January and February: Plant early spring crops.
March, April, and May: Plant spring crops.
June, July, and August: Plant summer crops.
September and October: Plant fall crops.
November and December: Plant winter crops.

The rest of this book offers gardening tips on individual vegetable crops and herbs, and their specific care requirements. The crops are grouped by season and also by taxonomic family.

Rotating Vegetable Families

Remember 5th- and 7th-grade science? Many of us memorized "King David (Phillip) Called Out For Good Spaghetti" to help us recall Kingdom, Division/Phylum, Class, Order, Family, Genus, Species. It is important to know the family that a particular group of plants belongs to, primarily because vegetables that are related to one another are likely to suffer damage from the same or similar insects, fungus, bacteria, and viruses (collectively termed "pests"). Vegetable family members are also likely to deplete the soil of the same specific nutrients required for growth. In smaller gardens and even on farms producing many acres of vegetables, a knowledgeable grower will rotate vegetable families between seasons. For instance, if you plant tomatoes in the spring, do not immediately follow in that same portion of the garden with a fall crop of potatoes or peppers; they are in the same family. Instead, switch that portion of the garden to a vegetable from another family, such as mustard greens. Do the same with container gardening—from season to season, switch vegetable families in the container to avoid depleting the soil of specific nutrients and to avoid building up pest populations.

Plant Spacing

In the following chapters, specific notes are made for each crop regarding plant spacing. When planting in the ground or in larger raised beds, you may plant individual crops in a single drill, double drill, or broadcast (see below). "Single drill" indicates a single row of vegetables planted down the center of the row. Generally, rows are 2–4 feet wide. "Double drill" refers to two rows of vegetables planted in that same 2–4 foot space in an offset pattern. "Broadcast" refers to scattering the seeds over the entire row in no particular pattern.

There are also notes for planting in containers. You might notice that I suggest spacing individual plants a bit closer in containers. This

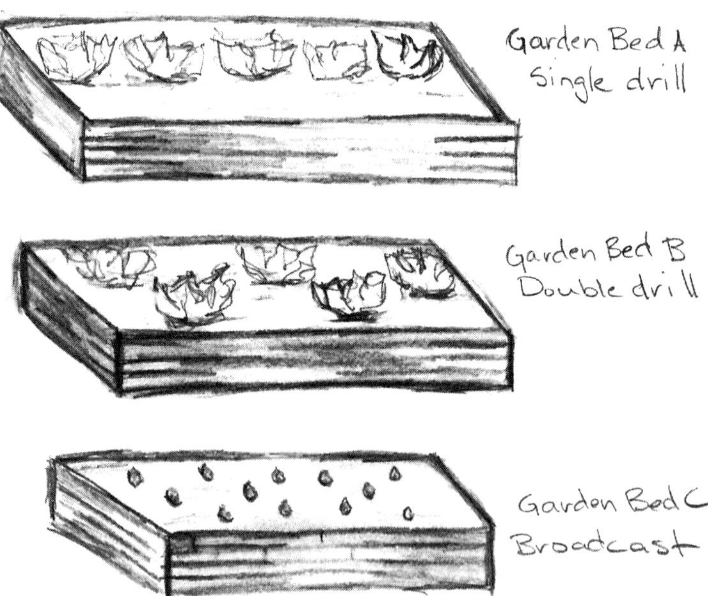

Planting patterns (drawing by Katie Goodlife)

is simply to allow a greater yield than one head or fruit from one plant for the entire garden. However, vegetable crops often do not grow as large in containers because of limited root space and therefore do not yield as much produce as plants growing in the ground or in larger raised beds. Many dwarf varieties of vegetables are available through seed companies. This is not to say you cannot grow standard varieties in containers; just be aware that you may not see the same yields as in a raised bed or in-ground garden.

Fertilizer Application

Each crop listed in the following chapters has preplant fertilizer application rates labeled as low, medium, or heavy. Refer to the fertilizer section of chapter 3 for clarification. Because readers may use different types of fertilizer, application rates are hard to provide. Therefore, I have listed the crops as low, medium, or heavy feeders. Remember, these preplant fertilizer application rates are for those gardeners growing edibles in in-ground gardens or for gardeners who have mixed native soil (even if just a little bit) with media or potting soil in raised-bed gardens. Gardeners growing in containers: you are most likely filling the container with a bagged potting soil. Bagged potting soils usually come "precharged," or with fertilizer incorporated. This means that you do not need to apply additional preplant fertilizer. If you use the same potting soil in the container season after season, then add preplant fertilizer the second season, or in year two. Every 2–3 years, replace the potting soil with fresh material.

Additionally, each crop listed has information regarding side-dress fertilizer applications. "Side-dressing" refers to fertilizing a crop after it has been actively growing in the garden. The term "side-dressing" is often used because gardeners apply the fertilizer to the side of the plant, around 6–8 inches from its base to avoid burning the plant. In containers, it is hard to side-dress with a granular fertilizer because of space limitations. Also, granular fertilizers often react differently with media (soilless soil) than they do with soil in a shallow raised bed or in-ground garden. Therefore, I suggest dissolving a liquid or water-soluble fertilizer with approximately 15% nitrogen (the first number on the bag or box N-P-K represents the nitrogen) in water and then pouring the solution into the container.

Another trick for fertilizing vegetables growing in containers is to incorporate a slow-release fertilizer into the container at the beginning of the season (preplant application) and avoid side-dressing altogether unless you see symptoms of nutrient deficiencies such as yellowing of the leaves. If you choose to incorporate a slow-release fertilizer, pay close attention to the length of time the fertilizer typically releases. For example, some slow-release products are labeled as releasing fertilizer over a 3–4 month period, whereas others release fertilizer for 9–12 months. Pick a slow-release fertilizer that covers the entire growing season for the crop you have in the container. As an example, a radish is usually ready to harvest within a month after planting. A 3–4 month slow-release fertilizer is suitable for this crop. But a tomato or pepper plant may grow for a couple of months before it begins to produce harvestable fruit. In this case, using at least a 5–6 month slow-release fertilizer is important to feed the plant throughout the season.

The other important piece of information to keep in mind when using slow-release fertilizers is that the time frame of release printed on the label is *very* weather dependent. Many fertilizer companies have estimated the release times based on an average air temperature of 70°F. You don't have to be an experienced gardener to know that very seldom is it a constant 70°F in Louisiana. Top that with our high humidity, and you can imagine how difficult it is to accurately estimate the amount of time the fertilizer is being released in the soil. So, err on choosing a slow-release fertilizer that extends beyond the normal growing season for the crop you are planting, especially when planting spring and summer crops.

Now that we have covered basic gardening techniques, let's dive into the fun part: individual crops and their specific care requirements. One more note: Each vegetable description is accompanied by a "Brief Glance" graphic, depicting important milestones in the life of the plant. Keep in mind that all day spans are approximate and weather dependent. Unusually hot or cool or wet periods will affect germination time, growth, and development, as well as harvest time.

6 SPRING AND SUMMER VEGETABLES

Spring and summer vegetables are grown in the warm season and generally after the last chance of frost has occurred. In South Louisiana the average last frost date is March 15, and in North Louisiana it is April 1. Of course, frost can end before or may occur slightly past these dates. Therefore, it is important to watch the local weather forecast to determine the ideal time to plant your spring garden each year. Warm-season vegetables cannot tolerate frost or freezes. If you plant early, be prepared to cover the vegetable crops. Light-colored sheets and frost-protection cloth work best.

It is somewhat more challenging to grow vegetables in the spring season than in the cool or fall season. This is due to the many insects and diseases that Louisiana gardeners must face in the warmer months. During this season, be prepared to spend at least two evenings or mornings each week inspecting the garden—pulling weeds and ridding the garden of pests. The work is worth the effort as spring and summer gardens are filled with a wonderful assortment of vegetables. Fresh tomatoes and cucumbers make fine additions to sandwiches, and the sweet crunchy texture of a watermelon, honeydew, or cantaloupe tastes great on a hot day.

Family Solanaceae

The family Solanaceae includes some of the more popular spring-planted vegetable crops, such as tomatoes, peppers, potatoes, and egg-plant. There is much folklore associated with this particular group of vegetables. When you're not working in the garden, run an internet search to learn more about the history of this family. The tomato in particular has a very interesting story. It was first known as an aphrodisiac and later thought poisonous. Yes, there are trace amounts of toxins in tomato foliage, but the average person would have to eat pounds of the foliage before becoming sick. There are much better options for salad bases . . . lettuce, kale, spinach, etc.!

EGGPLANT

Planting Dates

South Louisiana: March 15 through the end of June.
Central and North Louisiana: April 1 through the end of June.

Plant Spacing

Space eggplant 36 inches apart. Single drill only.

Typical Number of Plants on a 10-Foot Row

3 eggplant.

Plant Spacing in a Container

Plant only one eggplant per container. The bigger the container the better, for most vegetables and even more so for eggplant. This plant will absolutely require staking in the container. Eggplants can reach mature heights of 5–6 feet and the same width. I do not recommend planting an eggplant in any container less than 7 gallons in size.

Typical Fertilizer Requirements

In raised beds and in-ground gardens, apply a complete fertilizer such as 13-13-13 to the soil at a heavy rate one to three weeks prior to planting. Water in immediately. As with peppers and tomatoes, blooms continue setting upward as the plant grows. Apply a side-dress nitrogen fertilizer at first and third bloom set—around three weeks after planting and again three weeks after that. At each side-dressing, apply 1 to 2 teaspoons of a 15% nitrogen fertilizer per plant. Always water plants after applying fertilizer.

To side-dress one eggplant in a 7-gallon container, mix 1 tablespoon of a water-soluble 15% nitrogen fertilizer into a gallon of water. Pour the fertilizer solution into the container; avoid wetting the foliage. One gallon of solution is plenty of fertilizer to use per side-dress application. If the container is extremely wet, break this application into 2 applications 3–4 days apart.

Fertilize again if you ratoon the crop in the summer. "Ratooning" means to cut back a plant to 12–24 inches above ground level and allow the plant to regrow foliage and fruit. Eggplant that is cut back will continue to produce in the fall until the first killing freeze.

Insects of Concern

Aphids, whiteflies, flea beetles, stinkbugs, leaf-footed bugs.

Diseases of Concern

Downy mildew, powdery mildew.

A Brief Glance: Eggplant

Harvest Time

Harvest eggplant fruit when the skin is shiny. Eggplant fruit mature in a wide variety of colors and sizes depending on the variety chosen. They can be as small as a silver dollar or as large as a tear-shaped softball, and some are as long as a giant squash. Colors range from white to yellow, pink, purple, and green. Once seeds are fully developed, the fruit will taste bitter. It is better to harvest on the smaller, more immature side rather than large-sized fruit. Use pruning shears or a knife to cut eggplant from the shrub.

General Comments

Eggplants are a great filler vegetable. They can be sneaked into many recipes, enhancing the nutritional value of foods for picky eaters. For instance, add them to spaghetti sauce or lasagna dishes. Eggplant can be baked, grilled, fried, or sautéed. They can be both savory and sweet in flavor.

Grow at least one eggplant bush if your thumb is black. It will quickly turn green! These massive plants require staking but are worth the effort because they will produce from the spring well into the summer, and if ratooned in July or August will continue to produce until the first freeze. This is why planting a fall crop is not recommended.

Harvest eggplant often to encourage more production.

Toward the end of the season, if eggplant are loaded with aphids and whiteflies, it's best to remove them from the garden, as these pests will feast on newly transplanted fall crops. The eggplant are generally so large and robust that the insects cause little harm to them but will wreak havoc on small plants.

IRISH POTATOES

Planting Dates

Early spring potatoes

South Louisiana: Mid-January through February.

North Louisiana: Late January through the end of February.

Fall potatoes

Mid-August through mid-September.

Plant Spacing

Space potato seed pieces 9–12 inches apart.

Typical Number of Plants on a 10-Foot Row

10–12 potato plants.

Plant Spacing in a Container

In a typical 5-gallon container, plant up to 5 seed pieces.

Typical Fertilizer Requirements

In raised beds and in-ground gardens, apply a complete fertilizer such as 13-13-13 to the soil at a medium rate one to three weeks prior to planting. Water in immediately. Apply a side-dress nitrogen fertilizer when you first notice blooms and again two weeks later, when tubers are starting to develop. At each side-dressing, apply 1–2 teaspoons of a 15% nitrogen fertilizer per plant.

To side-dress potato plants in a 5-gallon container, mix 1 tablespoon of a water-soluble 15% nitrogen fertilizer into a gallon of water. Pour the fertilizer solution into the container; avoid wetting the foliage. One gallon of solution is plenty of fertilizer to use per side-dress application. If the container is extremely wet, break this application into 2 applications 3–4 days apart.

Insects of Concern

Nematodes, Colorado potato beetles, flea beetles.

Diseases of Concern

Rot.

A Brief Glance: Potatoes

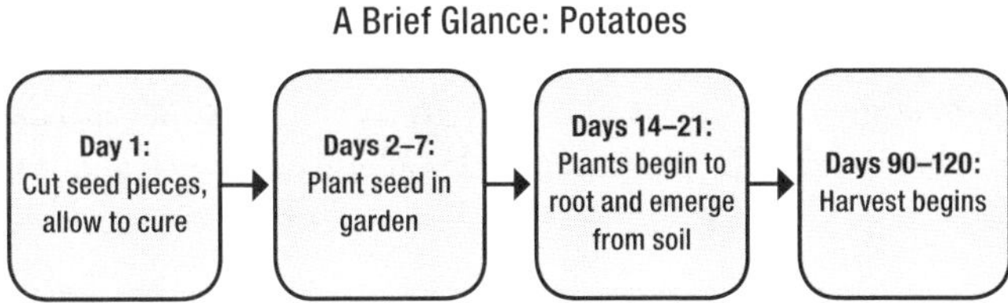

Harvest Time

Harvest potatoes when 50% or more of the plant tops have turned yellow or brown and have died. The skin on potatoes should not easily rub off when picking them from the soil. Lift potatoes out of the ground carefully with a pitchfork or shovel to avoid chopping when pulling them up. Most potatoes are ready to harvest 90–110 days after seeding. If heavy rains are anticipated toward the 90–100 day mark, harvest early to avoid rotting.

General Comments

Potatoes are a fun and easy crop to grow. Generally, if you don't plant too deep (only 4 or so inches below the soil line) and space them properly, you will be successful.

Cut seed potatoes in half or quarters. Technically only one eye is needed for germination, but in Louisiana's wet soils, smaller seed pieces will rot before germinating. Some gardeners cut the pieces a day or two prior to planting to help harden them off. You can also dust with a light application of sulfur by tossing the seed pieces in a paper bag with sulfur. This can also help you avoid rot and disease.

As flowers develop, you can begin checking regularly for tubers as they are now developing as well. Cover any tubers with extra soil from the side of the row or keep an extra bag of potting soil handy if you are growing potatoes in a container or raised bed. Tubers that are exposed to light will have green skin. The skin is green because an alkaloid called solanine has developed. Consuming potatoes with green skin will make your stomach hurt. Once a week, scout potatoes and make sure they are covered.

For the early spring planting, obtain seed potatoes from hardware stores and plant nurseries. In some cases, potatoes in the grocery store are sprayed with a chemical to prevent or delay them from sprouting. Farmer's markets are also great places to obtain seed stock for your own garden. Smaller potatoes harvested from the spring crop are excellent for use as seed pieces for planting a fall crop of potatoes. Keep potatoes in a dry, cool, dark location until you consume or replant them.

PEPPERS (BELL & HOT)

Planting Dates

Spring bell peppers

South Louisiana: Starting March 15.

Central and North Louisiana: Starting April 1.

Fall bell peppers

Mid-July through mid-August.

Spring hot peppers

South Louisiana: March 15 until the first week of June.

Central and North Louisiana: April 1 through the first week of June.

Plant Spacing

Space bell peppers at least 18–24 inches apart. Bell peppers can be double drilled to save space in smaller gardens. Space hot peppers 24–36 inches apart on rows. Single-drill hot peppers.

Typical Number of Plants on a 10-Foot Row

Bell peppers: 8–10 plants.

Hot peppers: 3–5 plants.

Plant Spacing in a Container

Plant 1 or 2 pepper plants per container. Container should be a minimum of 5 gallons. Larger containers are better.

Typical Fertilizer Requirements

In raised beds and in-ground gardens, apply a complete fertilizer such as 13-13-13 to the soil at a heavy rate one to three weeks prior to planting. Water in immediately. Apply a side-dress nitrogen fertilizer when you first notice blooms appearing and again when the third set of blooms appears on the plants. This is usually three weeks after planting and again three weeks later. At each side-dressing, apply 1–2 teaspoons of a 15% nitrogen fertilizer per plant.

To side-dress pepper plants in a 5-gallon container, mix 1 tablespoon of a water-soluble 15% nitrogen fertilizer into a gallon of water. Pour the fertilizer solution into the container; avoid wetting the foliage. One gallon of solution is plenty of fertilizer to use per side-dress application. If the container is extremely wet, break this application into 2 applications 3–4 days apart.

Insects of Concern

Aphids, stinkbugs, leaf-footed bugs, worms.

Diseases of Concern

Early blight, anthracnose, tomato spotted wilt virus (TSWV), bacterial leaf spot.

Harvest Time

Bell peppers come in a variety of shapes and sizes. Most sweet or bell peppers are 3- or 4-lobed and green. They generally are ready for harvest in 70–80 days. However, if you wait an additional 10–15 days, these peppers will mature into yellow, orange, purple and red colors. Be aware that waiting additional time may leave the fruit susceptible to additional insect and disease damage. Pepper fruit are ready for harvest when they easily twist or snap off the plant. If you have to wiggle or twist the pepper very hard and it tears away from the plant, it is not ready.

Hot peppers also range in color and size. They are typically harvested 70 days after planting. Hot peppers should fall off the plant with a brush of the hand. Those that cling to the plant can be left on a little longer to further mature. Larger peppers such as chili should be removed from the plant with pruners to avoid damaging stems. Peppers' flavor or intensity of heat is rated on a Scoville scale. The higher the number, the more pungency or heat you can expect.

A Brief Glance: Peppers

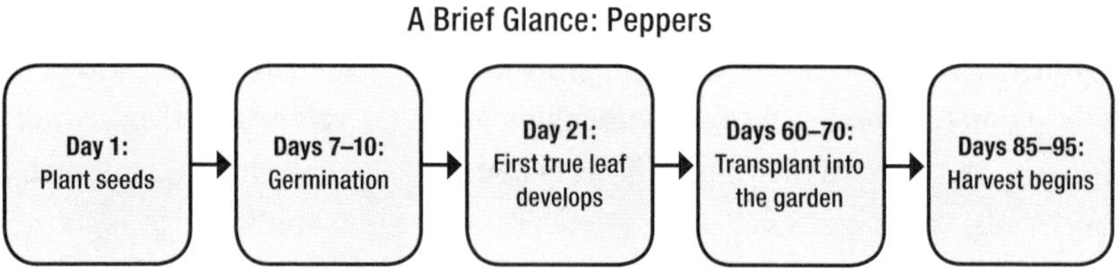

General Comments

Peppers are commonplace in Louisiana cuisine and therefore no garden should be without them. Like tomatoes, sweet peppers need to be staked, but they generally require much shorter trellis structures. Some hot peppers such as Tabasco become woody and do not require staking.

As the season progresses, size of the peppers will decrease, but they will also more readily change into mature colors. Green peppers are the easiest to grow, followed by purple peppers because they mature into their final color as they grow. Orange, red, and yellow peppers usually start green, grow into their full size, and then use an extra 10–15 days to mature into a ripe color. Of course, it is okay to harvest them green, but the purpose of planting a red, orange, or yellow pepper is to achieve the full ripe color. There are hundreds of varieties of peppers; try a few of each.

Many gardeners warn against planting sweet and hot peppers adjacent to one another because of a crossing of flavors. The fruit produced on a cross-pollinated pepper plant will look like the mother plant. For instance, if a hot pepper is planted next to a sweet pepper, the sweet pepper plant will not produce sweet peppers that are shaped like a hot pepper. The crossing happens in the seed. So yes, if you eat the fruit and seeds, you might experience a spicy sweet pepper. But if you remove the seeds from the fruit, the fruit will still taste sweet like the mother plant. Now, if those same seeds are saved and planted the following season, they are likely to have a crossed flavor.

Peppers can be started from seeds or purchased as transplants. If you choose to start seeds, plant seeds in small containers in a cold frame, greenhouse, or very bright windowsill 8–10 weeks prior to planting them into the garden.

TOMATOES

Planting Dates

Spring tomatoes

South Louisiana: Starting March 15.

Central and North Louisiana: Starting April 1.

Note: Some gardeners plant earlier than the spring dates listed. If you plant earlier, be prepared to cover if a freeze is in the forecast.

Summer tomatoes

May–June.

Fall tomatoes

Mid-July through early August.

Plant Spacing

Space tomatoes at least 18–24 inches apart. Single-drill on a row.

Typical Number of Plants on a 10-Foot Row

5–7 tomato plants.

Plant Spacing in a Container

Plant only one tomato plant per container. Container should be a minimum of 5 gallons. Larger containers are better. Determinate and dwarf tomato types do best in containers (see under "General Comments" below).

Typical Fertilizer Requirements

In raised beds and in-ground gardens, apply a complete fertilizer such as 13-13-13 to the soil at a heavy rate one to three weeks prior to planting. Water in immediately. Apply a side-dress nitrogen fertilizer at first and third bloom set. At each side-dressing, apply 1–2 teaspoons of a 15% nitrogen fertilizer per plant.

To side-dress tomato plants in a 5-gallon container, mix 1 tablespoon of a water-soluble 15% nitrogen fertilizer into a gallon of water. Pour the fertilizer solution into the container; avoid wetting the foliage. One gallon of solution is plenty of fertilizer to use per side-dress application. If the container is extremely wet, break this application into 2 applications 3–4 days apart.

Calcium nitrate is a good fertilizer to use when side-dressing. The extra calcium can help prevent blossom-end rot, especially when gardening in containers. Always water plants after fertilizing.

Insects of Concern

Aphids, whiteflies, thrips, leaf miners, stinkbugs, leaf-footed bugs, worms, snails.

Diseases of Concern

Early blight, anthracnose, tomato spotted wilt virus (TSWV), timber rot, soft rots.

Harvest Time

Tomatoes can be harvested anytime after breaker point (a slight yellow to orange color blushing on the fruit). Typically, home and market gardeners wait for the fruit to fully ripen. Fruit colors range from ivory to pink, red, yellow, orange, and purplish black depending on the variety selected.

A Brief Glance: Tomatoes

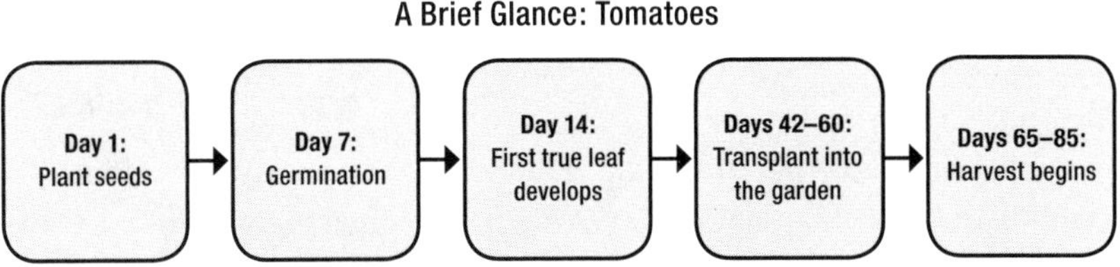

General Comments

Tomatoes are the most popular of all vegetables grown in small gardens. They can be started from seeds or purchased as transplants.

Spring-planted tomatoes are the easiest to grow. There is less insect and disease pressure on spring-planted tomatoes compared to summer- and fall-planted crops.

It is fine to wait until mid-March or April 1 and simply purchase tomato transplants from the plant nursery or hardware store. However, if you desire a particular variety or want an extra-large plant to place into the ground at the beginning of the season, starting plants from seeds is your option. Plant the seeds in small containers 8–10 weeks prior to planting them into the garden. Keep the seedlings in a cold frame, greenhouse, or a bright windowsill.

Tomatoes are very sensitive to cool temperatures, and a late frost or freeze is likely to delay harvest if not kill your plant.

If you are purchasing small seedlings (transplants), plant them into the garden soil at the same depth as the root ball that was removed from the container. Planting deep is only necessary if the seedling is extremely "leggy" (the plant appears very tall and cannot support itself). Otherwise, planting deeper does not help growth.

Stake tomatoes the same day or at least the same week that you plant the seedlings in the ground. Tomato cages work well for a few plants; for multiple plants, consider purchasing wooden or metal stakes and tying the plants with twine directly to the stakes. There are almost as many different staking and trellising methods as there are gardeners—there really is no right or wrong way to support the plant as long as it is not left to support itself. Once loaded with fruit, the branches break easily if not supported. Gardeners grow tomatoes along fences, in cages, in homemade hoops, on laundry dry lines, and in multiple other ways. Just remember, when you are tying the twine around the branches or main stem, don't tie too tight; doing so will cut off the vascular flow of nutrients and water throughout the plant and the top will eventually die.

There are two types of tomatoes, indeterminate and determinate. Indeterminate tomatoes continue to grow because their terminal growing point is a leaf bud, whereas determinate or bush-type tomatoes stop growing at 3–4 feet because their terminal bud is a flower. Indeterminate tomatoes can reach 12-plus feet, requiring much taller cages or stakes. If your tomato plant starts to resemble Jack's beanstalk, there is no reason you cannot cut off the top. Doing so will not hurt the plant. Alternatively, continue to let it grow but figure out a way to keep staking it higher and higher.

Spray a copper-based fungicide (carefully following labeled directions) at the base of all tomato plants for two to three weeks after planting them in the garden. This will help protect the plant against early blight. Early blight is one of those diseases we can just about bet on occurring throughout Louisiana. For most crops, I do not recommend preventative spraying, but in the case of tomatoes it's important. Early blight starts at the base of the plant, working its way upward. Small-to-large target-like spots show up on the leaves and multiply quickly until the entire leaf appears brown and the plant starts to defoliate. Why is this a problem? Because plants need foliage to photosynthesize so they have enough energy to produce fruit, and the fruit that is produced must be protected by foliage so that it does not get burned or scalded by excessive sunlight. Too much sun causes a white patch on the tomato's skin that never ripens.

Entire hosts of diseases and viruses can occur later in the season, but it's best to identify those diseases first and then determine if you want to spray pesticides for control.

Patio gardeners love growing tomatoes in pots. Remember, the larger the container, the better. If you water too much, you will greatly increase blossom-end rot on your tomato plants. Blossom-end rot occurs when the bottom of the tomato collapses and turns black due to a calcium deficiency. There may be a lack of this element in the soil, or you may be leaching too much out of the soil by over-watering. Blossom-end rot can also be caused by wet and dry cycling from inconsistent irrigation.

Note: In indeterminate tomatoes, the taller you allow the plant to grow, the more likely higher-produced fruit will have blossom-end rot. It is hard for calcium to move higher and higher in the plant. If the portion of the tomato that is black and rotting is not on the bottom or blossom end of the fruit, it is a disease. Bring to your local LSU AgCenter county agent for identification and for management options.

Family Cucurbitaceae

In most cucurbit crops, the male flowers generally develop first. Do not worry when these flowers fall off and do not produce fruit. However, if both male and female flowers are present and fruit is still not forming or aborting early, something is not right.

Do you see bees, flies, or wasps in the garden? If not, plant herbs or flowers to attract pollinators. Allow herbs to go to flower so pollinators will visit. If pollinators are present, tap cucurbit flowers and inspect for small insects. These insects may be feeding on the flowers and disrupting pollination. I generally do not like spraying cucurbits heavily with insecticides because they are so dependent on pollinators for fruit production. It is best to apply light horticultural oils if early in the season or insecticidal soaps if you see aphids or thrips in the flowers. Another potential reason for lack of fruit production is extremely hot weather. Extreme heat can damage pollen.

Hand pollination is achievable in small gardens. Simply transfer pollen from a male flower to a female flower using a cotton swab or small paintbrush. The pollen is a dusty yellow substance that forms on the anthers of a male flower. This pollen must be transferred to the stigma, or center sticky portion, of the female flower. A male flower will not have an enlarged ovary behind the bloom; a female flower will have a visible enlarged ovary that looks like a miniature cucumber, squash, or melon.

Signs your cucurbit crop is not properly pollinated:

- Fruit abortion.
- Misshaped fruit.

Signs your cucurbit crop was over-fertilized:

- No flowers are being formed, even well into the season.
- Plants have very dense foliage.
- Fruit tastes watery (this can also occur if you over-water the plants).

If cooler spring weather is predicted, wait a little later to plant cucurbits as they are more sensitive to cold than other warm-season crops.

CANTALOUPE

Planting Dates

South Louisiana: March 15 through August 1.

Central and North Louisiana: April 1 through mid-July.

Plant Spacing

Space cantaloupe plants 24–36 inches apart. Single-drill the row and consider skipping the next row to allow the plants enough space to vine out.

Typical Number of Plants on a 10-Foot Row

3, maybe 4 cantaloupe plants.

Plant Spacing in a Container

Plant one cantaloupe plant in a 5-gallon container. If you are using a larger container, two plants may be appropriate, especially if vines are trellised. Chicken wire, tomato cages, and homemade trellises are all fine. The vine must have something to climb, and the fruit must be supported. Knee-high stockings or any inexpensive cloth can be used to support growing fruit. Simply tie the cloth in a sling fashion and attach it to a sturdy trellis. If growing cantaloupe in containers, choose varieties that produce smaller fruit, such as Ambrosia.

Typical Fertilizer Requirements

In raised beds and in-ground gardens, apply a complete fertilizer such as 13-13-13 to the soil at a medium rate one to three weeks prior to planting. Water in immediately. Apply a side-dress nitrogen fertilizer at first bloom set and once more a week later. At each side-dressing, apply 1–2 teaspoons of a 15% nitrogen fertilizer per plant.

To side-dress one cantaloupe in a 5-gallon container, mix 1 tablespoon of a water-soluble 15% nitrogen fertilizer into a gallon of water. Pour the fertilizer solution into the container; avoid wetting the foliage. One gallon of solution is plenty of fertilizer to use per side-dress application. If the container is extremely wet, break this application into 2 applications 3–4 days apart.

Insects of Concern

Aphids, cucumber beetles, stinkbugs, leaf-footed bugs, worms.

Diseases of Concern

Downy mildew, powdery mildew, cucumber mosaic virus.

Harvest Time

Canteloupe should easily slip from the vine. In other words, take the fruit and hang it in the crook of your finger—does it fall off? If so, it's ready to harvest; if not and you can swing it, the fruit is not ready. There should be a slight musky sweet smell and the netting should be fully developed (skin feels rough, not smooth).

A Brief Glance: Canteloupe

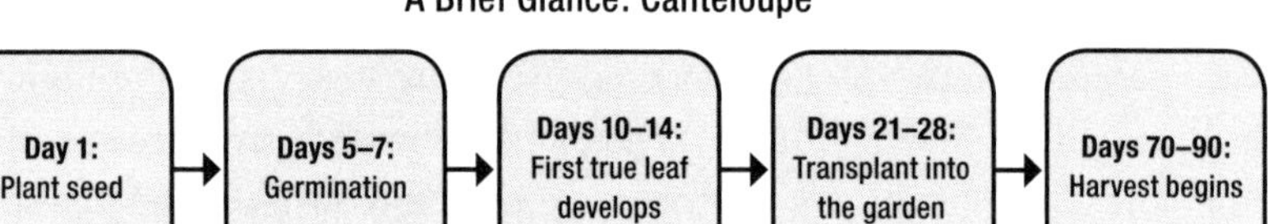

General Comments

Cantaloupe can be grown in very small gardens by simply allowing the vine to trail out of the raised bed or by growing in an extra-large container (at least 10–15 gallons) and trellising on a balcony railing or other trellis structure. If you are trellising cantaloupe, be prepared to support the weight of the fruit with scraps of cloth or knee-high pantyhose.

If you are growing cantaloupe in the ground, ensure that the garden has adequate drainage. The fruit will quickly rot if left sitting in standing water. You can always place a sheet of cardboard or plastic underneath fruit in direct contact with the soil.

CUCUMBERS

Planting Dates

Spring cucumbers

South Louisiana: Starting March 15.

Central and North Louisiana: Starting April 1.

Fall cucumbers

July through early August.

Plant Spacing

Space cucumber plants 12–36 inches apart. If you single-drill cucumbers along a trellis, use the tighter spacing. If you do not plan to trellis your cucumbers, allow more space between plants.

Typical Number of Plants on a 10-Foot Row

7–10 cucumber plants.

Plant Spacing in a Container

Plant 2 cucumbers per container. Container should be a minimum of 5 gallons. Larger containers are better. Make sure you have some idea of how you will stake cucumbers in containers. Tomato cages work fine. Or, get more creative with decorative trellises or build your own.

Typical Fertilizer Requirements

In raised beds and in-ground gardens, apply a complete fertilizer such as 13-13-13 to the soil at a medium rate one to three weeks prior to planting. Water in immediately. Apply a side-dress nitrogen fertilizer starting at the first bloom and again weekly for up to three weeks. At each side-dressing, apply 1–2 teaspoons of a 15% nitrogen fertilizer per plant.

To side-dress cucumbers in a 5-gallon container, mix 1 tablespoon of a water-soluble 15% nitrogen fertilizer into a gallon of water. Pour the fertilizer solution into the container; avoid wetting the foliage. One gallon of solution is plenty of fertilizer to use per side-dress application. If the container is extremely wet, break this application into 2 applications 3–4 days apart.

Insects of Concern

Aphids, cucumber beetles, stinkbugs, leaf-footed bugs, snails and slugs (if you do not trellis).

Diseases of Concern

Downy mildew, powdery mildew, anthracnose, cucumber mosaic virus.

Harvest Time

Once cucumbers start to produce, check the vines at least three times a week. There are several types of cucumbers: pickling, slicers, and burpless. The pickling types should be 2–4 inches in length and 1/2–1 inch in diameter. Slicers should be 6–7 inches in length and no more than 2 inches in diameter. Burpless cucumbers will be much longer—up to 18 inches with a diameter of 1 1/2 to 2 inches. Cucumber skin should be dark green. When skin starts to yellow and the fruit has greatly widened, just throw it in the compost bin because it will taste bitter.

A Brief Glance: Cucumbers

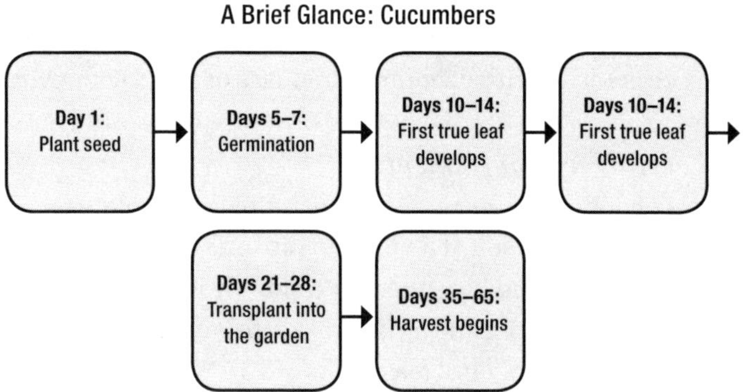

General Comments

Want to spark some friendly competition among your family, friends, or neighbors? Have each gardener plant a cucumber vine or two. Weekly, each contestant should weigh their fruit, and the person who produced the most cucumbers at the end of the season gets a prize!

My husband and I were so fascinated by our cucumber harvest one year that we actually recorded the weight of each harvest and charted it on the refrigerator. I guess this makes us "garden nerds," but it was so exciting to see if we beat the previous week's harvest and just as exciting to watch our total pound numbers climb.

Trellising is not absolutely necessary but helps tremendously. Trellising allows you to more easily see fruit ready for harvest, encourages fruit to grow straighter, and reduces the chance of yellow belly (a yellowing of the portion of skin in contact with the ground). Plus, trellising helps keep snails and slugs off fruit.

Do not wait too many days after cucumbers start to mature to check the garden. They will literally grow overnight and become bitter quickly.

Look up new recipes and think about pickling if you grow ten or more plants. . . . You'll need lots of hungry mouths to feed or a great alternative for prolonging the storage life of this rather perishable but delicious vegetable crop.

Even though there is a pickling type of cucumber, you can also pickle a burpless or slicing cucumber.

GOURDS & PUMPKINS

Planting Dates

Mid-June to early July (for a Halloween harvest) through August (for a Thanksgiving harvest). Plantings can continue through September but will produce much later.

Plant Spacing

Space bush-type pumpkins 3 feet apart and vining types up to 6 feet apart. Consider skipping the adjacent row when planting vining types. Allow vines to overlap to prevent sunscald—a blemish that develops on the fruit where it is directly exposed to sunlight and not covered by foliage.

Typical Number of Plants on a 10-Foot Row

2–3 pumpkin plants.

Plant Spacing in a Container

Pumpkins are best suited to in-ground gardens and raised beds. However, several bush varieties are on the market. One bush-type pumpkin plant is suitable per 10-gallon container or larger.

Typical Fertilizer Requirements

In raised beds and in-ground gardens, apply a complete fertilizer such as 13-13-13 to the soil at a heavy rate one to three weeks prior to planting. Water in immediately. Apply a side-dress nitrogen fertilizer at first bloom set and again at weekly increments for two additional weeks. At each side-dressing, apply 1–2 teaspoons of a 15% nitrogen fertilizer per plant.

To side-dress one bush-type plant in a 10-gallon container, mix 1 tablespoon of a water-soluble 15% nitrogen fertilizer into a gallon of water. Pour the fertilizer solution into the container; avoid wetting the foliage. One gallon of solution is plenty of fertilizer to use per side-dress application. If the container is extremely wet, break this application into 2 applications 3–4 days apart.

Insects of Concern

Aphids, worms and loopers, snails, slugs.

Diseases of Concern

Downy mildew, powdery mildew, anthracnose.

Harvest Time

Pumpkin and gourd skin should be tough and not easily penetrated by your fingernail. The color should be fully developed but, depending on variety, ranges from white to silver, pale orange, coral, dark orange, and variegated for gourds.

A Brief Glance: Gourds and Pumpkins

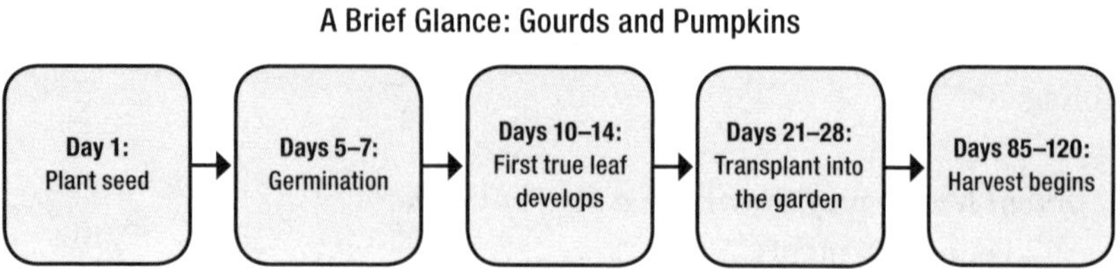

General Comments

Pumpkins are a fun crop to grow but *very* challenging for beginning and even experienced gardeners. This is the one crop that I consider extremely hard to manage sustainably or even organically in Louisiana. Our humidity and insect pressure can devastate this crop overnight. So be diligent in checking the garden often. Watch out particularly for worms and loopers, caterpillars, slugs, and snails. Apply a control method quickly if you see them.

If you lose all of the foliage early from insect or disease damage, harvest the pumpkins and store them in a dark, cool, dry location until you are ready to consume them or use them for decoration.

Smaller-sized pumpkins tend to produce better in Louisiana than larger, jack-o'-lantern types. Two of my favorite larger pumpkins are actually squash: the Cinderella variety is squat and ranges in color from pale yellow to dark orange, and Silver Moon, also squat in shape, ranges from white to dark gray or silver. When ordering pumpkin seed, look for varieties that are resistant to downy mildew and powdery mildew.

SQUASH (SUMMER & WINTER)

Planting Dates

South Louisiana: March 15 through mid-August.

Central and North Louisiana: April 1 through late July.

Plant Spacing

Plant vining types one foot apart and bush types 3 feet apart.

Typical Number of Plants on a 10-Foot Row

Vining types: Up to 10. Bush types: 3.

Plant Spacing in a Container

Read the tag on the seedling container or read the seed package. Bush-type squash do best when only one is planted per 5-gallon container. For vining-type squash, plant 2 per 5-gallon container. Be prepared to stake vining squash planted in a container. Again, 5 gallons is the minimum-size container that should be used for squash.

Typical Fertilizer Requirements

In raised beds and in-ground gardens, apply a complete fertilizer such as 13-13-13 to the soil one to three weeks prior to planting. Water in immediately. Apply a side-dress nitrogen fertilizer weekly for at least three weeks after plants start to bloom. At each side-dressing, apply 1–2 teaspoons of a 15% nitrogen fertilizer per plant.

To side-dress squash in a 5-gallon container, mix 1 tablespoon of a water-soluble 15% nitrogen fertilizer into a gallon of water. Pour the fertilizer solution into the container; avoid wetting the foliage. One gallon of solution is plenty of fertilizer to use per side-dress application. If the container is extremely wet, break this application into 2 applications 3–4 days apart.

Insects of Concern

Aphids, cucumber beetles, whiteflies, stinkbugs, leaf-footed bugs, snails, slugs.

Diseases of Concern

Anthracnose, downy mildew, powdery mildew.

Harvest Time

Summer squash will have tender skins easily pierced by your fingernail. They will be white or yellow and should be harvested on the smaller side, before seeds have fully developed. Over-mature summer squash are bitter. Generally, they should be no more than 2–3 inches in diameter and 4 or so inches in length.

Winter squash are planted at the same time as summer squash but store for a much longer period of time. Winter squash will have a hard shell. They range in shapes, sizes, and colors, often looking more like gourds and pumpkins. There are hundreds of varieties of both summer and winter squash, and almost all do well in Louisiana.

A Brief Glance: Squash

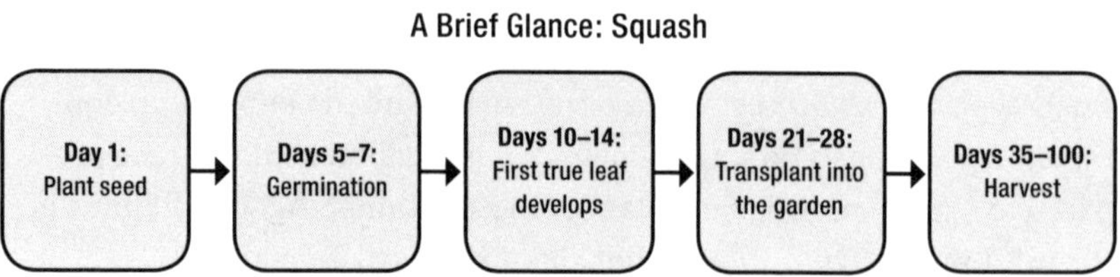

General Comments

All types of squash tend to be heavy producers. Check your plants often as squash can become over-mature almost overnight. In the case of summer squash, the larger the squash is, the more bitter it will taste. Pick immature for summer squash and mature for winter squash.

If plants are robust and producing well but older, lower foliage starts to brown and fall off, this is most likely nothing to concern yourself with. As these larger leaves become damaged, they also become susceptible to secondary fungus, which only attacks dead or decaying tissue. Removing these leaves is fine.

Squash can be prickly, especially the stems. Wear gloves if you are sensitive.

WATERMELON

Planting Dates

South Louisiana: Mid- to late March through August 1.

Central and North Louisiana: April 1 through the end of July.

Plant Spacing

A single watermelon vine has the potential to cover 10 feet by 10 feet. This does not mean they need to be planted that far apart. Overlapping of vines actually helps protect fruit from sunburn. In a smaller garden, a watermelon vine can be planted at the edge of a raised bed and allowed to creep over the grass. In an in-ground garden, space plants at least 4 feet apart in the row and consider skipping the adjacent row.

Typical Number of Plants on a 10-Foot Row

2 to 3 watermelon plants.

Plant Spacing in a Container

Watermelons grow best when they have plenty of space to spread. Varieties that produce large-sized melons (10 lbs. and greater) should be planted in an in-ground garden or raised bed. Mini- or personal-sized melons (2–6 lbs.) can be planted in large containers (10 gallons or larger), one vine per container. Treat the mini-melons the same as you would if you were growing cantaloupe in a container. Look for seed companies that cater to the home gardener. Watermelon varieties come and go almost as quickly as the season changes, but there are several varieties developed for the container grower.

Typical Fertilizer Requirements

In raised beds and in-ground gardens, apply a complete fertilizer such as 13-13-13 to the soil at a medium rate one to three weeks prior to planting. Water in immediately. Apply a side-dress nitrogen fertilizer at first bloom set and again a week after (this normally occurs when vines go from a bush form to a vining or running form). At each side-dressing, apply 1–2 teaspoons of a 15% nitrogen fertilizer per plant.

To side-dress one personal-sized melon in a 10-gallon container, mix 1 tablespoon of a water-soluble 15% nitrogen fertilizer into a gallon of water. Pour the fertilizer solution into the container; avoid wetting the foliage. One gallon of solution is plenty of fertilizer to use per side-dress application. If the container is extremely wet, break this application into 2 applications 3–4 days apart.

Watermelon should not be fertilized too late in the season. If the melons are developed, avoid fertilizing unless the vines are yellowing. The more fertilizer applied, the lower the sugar content will be and your watermelon will have a bland flavor.

Insects of Concern

Cucumber beetles, snails, slugs.

Diseases of Concern

Gummy stem blight, anthracnose, Fusarium wilt, downy mildew, powdery mildew, watermelon mosaic virus.

Harvest Time

Watermelon rind color must be fully developed prior to harvest. Some melons have a stripe pattern, whereas other varieties are all one color. Make sure there is a distinct color to the rind. The bottom portion of the rind in contact with the ground must be pale to dark yellow prior to harvest. Often, but not always, the tendril closest to the fruit will be dried and brown. Some gardeners thump the melon. It should sound hollow, like thumping your throat. Also take note of the variety of watermelon you planted. Some mature at 5–8 lbs. while others easily reach the 40-lb. mark. Knowing the mature size of your variety helps tremendously. The seed package or transplant label should provide you with a mature weight. Harvesting watermelons is something that comes with practice. Don't be in too much of a hurry; if the interior flesh is pale pink, you can't reattach it to the vine. It won't continue to ripen if picked too early. Most melons are ready 60–80 days after planting.

A Brief Glance: Watermelon

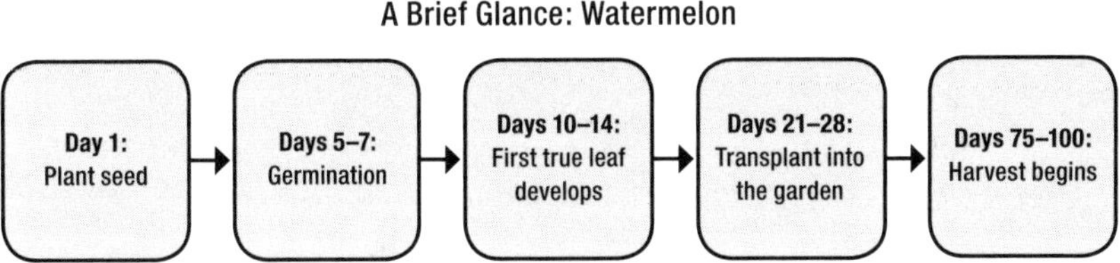

General Comments

Watermelon is the most delicious crop to grow in a vegetable garden. Don't fret if you think they require too large of a space; just grow one vine at the side of a raised bed and allow it to spread into the grass.

Think you'll waste more than you will eat? Plant personal-sized melons that are 5–8 lbs. in mature weight. But trust me, of all crops to have excessive amounts of, watermelons are the easiest to give away. Plus, you'll make friends for life!

What makes a watermelon taste so good is the combination of its texture and sweetness. Avoid over-watering and over-fertilizing this crop to keep texture and sweetness in balance. After the vine begins to run, shut off the irrigation, only watering if there hasn't been rain in ten days or more.

Fix drainage problems in the garden to avoid melons sitting in standing water. Cardboard can be place underneath melons to reduce rot.

After vines have started to run, don't be too worried about weed control. Weeds can help melons by shading them and reducing sunburn.

Are you attempting to plant seedless watermelons? Plant a few with seeds too, as seedless watermelons are poor pollinators and often require a seeded watermelon for proper pollination to occur.

Family Leguminosae ("Legumes")

The legume family includes beans, peas, and even clover. Clover is often considered a weed, but some gardeners purposely plant it as a cover crop. A really neat thing about legumes is that they actually fix nitrogen in the air and make it available in the soil for plant growth. Nitrogen fixation is when legumes absorb nitrogen from the air and convert it to an available form that plants can use. Legumes are a good choice to plant between seasons of tomatoes, cucumbers, and other popular crops. Within the bean portion of the legume family, gardeners usually grow one of two types of beans, snap beans or lima beans.

What is the difference between snap beans and lima beans? Snap beans produce narrow, long pods that are eaten whole. Think of your typical "green bean" or yellow wax bean. Snap beans are planted earlier than lima beans.

Lima beans, often referred to as "butter beans" in the South, are shelled. The pods are usually not eaten. Lima beans need warmer soils to germinate, grow, and produce as compared to snap beans.

To complicate matters more (at least for those who are new at growing beans), you can grow bush- or pole-type varieties of both snap and lima beans.

What is the difference between bush and pole beans?

Bush beans:

- Produce a lot of pods in a short time frame.
- Take up more space in the garden, because they grow wide rather than up.
- Have relatively little trouble with pests and diseases (because of short harvest time).

Pole beans:

- Are a vertical space saver—they climb up trellises and tepees.
- Are more susceptible to pests and diseases because they continue to bear, slowly, throughout the summer as insect and disease populations rise.

EDAMAME

Edamame is the name commonly used for food-grade soybeans. Commercially cultivated soybeans are grown thousands of acres at a time and usually dried on the plant to later harvest for the manufacturing of cooking oils, plastics, crayons, makeup, and so on. Edamame is not allowed to dry on the plant (unless you are trying to save seeds). It is harvested green and usually steamed in the shell, with the individual beans pushed out of the shell for consumption.

This bean became popular with the rise of sushi and hibachi bars and restaurants. It is easy to grow and delicious. Our family enjoys them as a snack!

Planting Dates

South Louisiana: Direct seed edamame into the garden mid-March through June.

Central and North Louisiana: Wait until April 1 to plant seeds. Edamame prefers warmer soils for optimum germination.

Plant Spacing

Plant edamame seed every 4–8 inches. Varieties available for home gardeners are bush types, so trellising isn't necessary.

Typical Number of Plants on a 10-Foot Row

12–35 edamame plants.

Plant Spacing in a Container

Limit edamame plants to 3 per 5-gallon container.

Typical Fertilizer Requirements

In raised beds and in-ground gardens, apply a complete fertilizer such as 13-13-13 to the soil at a low rate at least one week prior to planting the bean seeds. Water in immediately. Do not side-dress edamame unless it is showing signs of nutrient deficiency, such as yellowing at the base of the plant.

Insects of Concern

Stinkbugs, leaf-footed bugs.

Diseases of Concern

Anthracnose, mosaic virus, Fusarium wilt, Cercospora leaf spot, several rots, rust.

Harvest Time

Harvest edamame when the pods are dark green and the beans begin to bulge beneath the pod. Check your edamame crop every 3–4 days after the plants begin to produce. Pods will quickly become yellow and the quality weakens. Harvest generally occurs 75–85 days after planting.

A Brief Glance: Edamame

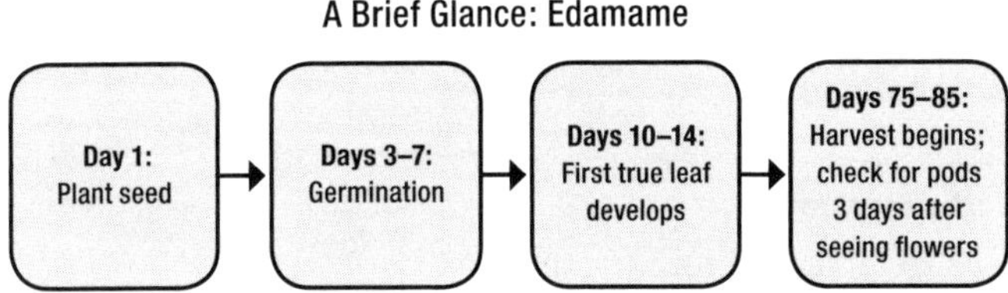

General Comments

Refrigerate edamame after harvesting. To increase shelf life, blanch and freeze the beans for use throughout the year.

ENGLISH PEAS

Love to eat peas but hate to shell them? This delicate little edible is eaten in the pod. Sugar snaps require a fence or trellis to grow on.

Planting Dates

Early spring

Direct seed English peas mid-December through the end of January.

Fall English peas

Direct seed English peas in September.

Plant Spacing

Plant English peas along a trellis every 3–6 inches and no more than 1/2 inch deep.

Typical Number of Plants on a 10-Foot Row

20–36 pea plants.

Plant Spacing in a Container

Plant 6–8 pea seeds in a 5-gallon container. Place a trellis of some sort in the container when seedlings are small.

Typical Fertilizer Requirements

In raised beds and in-ground gardens, apply a complete fertilizer such as 13-13-13 to the soil at a low rate at least one week prior to planting the pea seeds. Do not side-dress unless peas are showing signs of nutrient deficiency.

Insects of Concern

Aphids, beetles, leaf miners, thrips.

Diseases of Concern

Powdery mildew, several rots, bacterial blight.

Harvest Time

Harvest English peas when pods are still flat but the seed slightly bulges from the pod. Harvest usually occurs 55–70 days after planting. Visit the garden every two to three days after harvest begins to pick pods before they become over-mature.

A Brief Glance: English peas

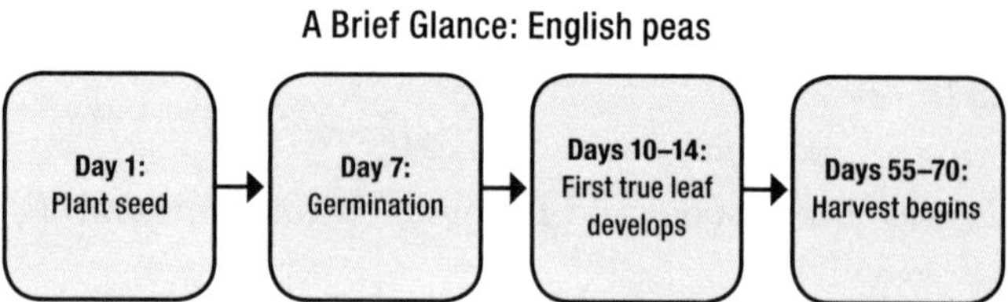

General Comments

Successional plantings may help you increase the harvest period for

English peas. Do not forget to trellis these peas, and try them in a variety of dishes!

LIMA OR BUTTER BEANS

Planting Dates

Spring lima or butter beans

Direct seed beans into the garden mid-March through June.

Fall lima or butter beans

Direct seed beans into the garden July through early September.

Plant Spacing

Space bush lima beans 3–6 inches apart and pole lima beans 6–12 inches apart. Generally, 2–3 seeds are placed in each hole for pole limas, but only 1 or 2 seeds for bush limas.

Typical Number of Plants on a 10-Foot Row

10–20 plants depending on bush versus pole types.

Plant Spacing in a Container

Plant 4–6 seeds or small seedlings of bush lima beans or 2–3 pole-type lima beans per 5-gallon container. Plan to trellis vining lima beans.

Typical Fertilizer Requirements

In raised beds and in-ground gardens, apply a complete fertilizer such as 13-13-13 to the soil at a low rate at least one week prior to planting the bean seeds. Do not side-dress lima beans unless they are stressed. Beans are sensitive to over-fertilization and will not set flowers or pods if they receive too much nitrogen fertilizer.

Insects of Concern

Aphids, cucumber beetles, stinkbugs, leaf-footed bugs.

Diseases of Concern

Anthracnose, mosaic virus, Cercospora leaf spot, several rots, rust.

Harvest Time

Harvest lima beans when the pods are 3 to 4 inches in length and a bulge can be seen. (This is the opposite of snaps, which should be long without bulges.) Allowing them to dry (generally overnight) helps them shell out easier. Store in an airtight container or plastic bag and cool immediately after shelling. Bush-type lima beans generally require 60–65 days from planting to harvesting, whereas pole lima beans need 70–90 days.

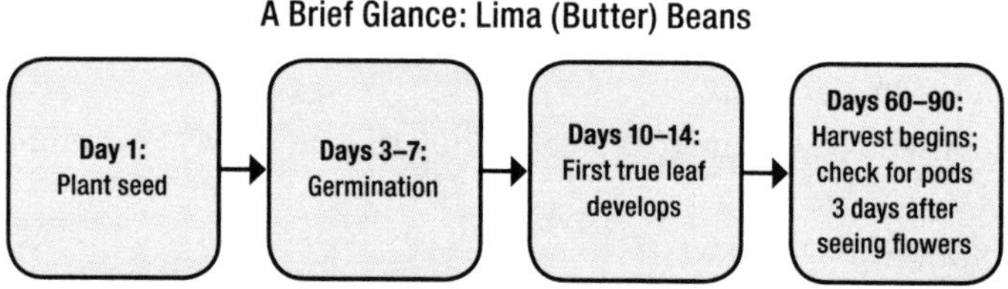

General Comments

Lima beans are a true delight in certain portions of the state. I am particularly fond of these delicious beans when accompanied by smothered chicken with rice and cold shredded cabbage tossed in oil and vinegar.

SNAP BEANS

Planting Dates

Spring snap beans

Direct seed snap beans into the garden mid-February through mid-May.

Fall snap beans

Direct seed snap beans into the garden mid-August through mid-September.

Plant Spacing

Space bush-type snap bean seed 2–3 inches apart and pole-type snap bean seed 12 inches apart. Only plant twice as deep as the seed is wide—no deeper than 1/2 inch for both types of snap beans.

Typical Number of Plants on a 10-Foot Row

10 pole snap beans or about 40 bush snap beans, planting on a single drill.

Plant Spacing in a Container

Plant 4 seeds or small seedlings of bush snap beans or 2 pole-type snap beans per 5-gallon container. If using larger containers, you can add up to 6 bush snap beans or 3 vining snap beans per container. Plan to trellis vining snap beans.

Typical Fertilizer Requirements

In raised beds and in-ground gardens, apply a complete fertilizer such as 13-13-13 to the soil at a low rate at least one week prior to planting the snap beans. Only side-dress snap beans if they show signs of stress. Over-fertilizing beans will result in bushy plants with tremendous foliage but no flower or pod set.

Insects of Concern

Aphids, worms, thrips, leaf miners, whiteflies, stinkbugs.

Diseases of Concern

Anthracnose, Alternaria leaf spot, several types of rot, bacterial blight, mosaic virus.

A Brief Glance: Snap Beans

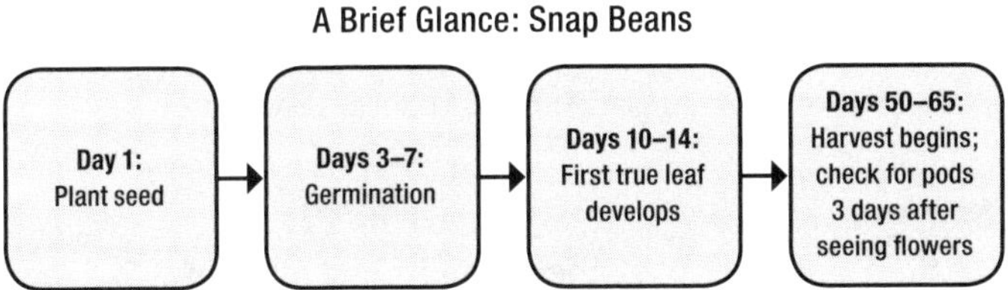

Harvest Time

Harvest snap beans when they are firm enough to snap but big bulges aren't showing through the pod. This generally occurs a couple of weeks after the bloom. Bush snap beans are easy to pull from plants, whereas pole snap beans are a little harder and might require scissors to successfully remove the pods without destroying the plant. Beans mature very quickly; once you start harvesting, be prepared to visit the garden for a harvest every two to three days. Bush snap beans are generally ready 50–55 days after planting. Pole snap beans take a little longer, requiring 60–65 days before production.

General Comments

Pole snap beans will harvest for a longer period than bush snap beans. But pole beans require a fence or a trellis. Many gardeners grow pole beans on a tepee-style trellis. These are fun to build but must be pushed at least 1 1/2–2 feet into the ground to support the vines. Obtain help when pulling out the tepee trellis so you don't injure your back! Or leave it in year-round.

Have bamboo? This plant makes an excellent bean trellis post. Just be sure to cut the bamboo and allow it to dry for several weeks prior to posting in the vegetable garden. If you don't, you'll actually be propagating the bamboo right into your vegetable garden!

Snap beans are generally consumed whole, pod and all.

SOUTHERN PEAS

The Southern pea is more like a black-eyed pea but can also have a purple or pink eye. Central and northern Louisiana natives drool for this veggie crop!

Planting Dates

Direct seed Southern peas March 1 through August.

Plant Spacing

Space Southern peas 6–12 inches apart and plant only 1/2 inch deep. Use closer spacing for bush types. If you choose a vining type, use the 12-inch spacing.

Typical Number of Plants on a 10-Foot Row

10–24 pea plants.

Plant Spacing in a Container

Seed a 5-gallon container with up to 9 Southern pea seeds, but thin emerging seedlings to 3 to 4 plants. Lots of little critters enjoy eating pea seeds, so I often over-plant seed and thin later.

Typical Fertilizer Requirements

In raised beds and in-ground gardens, apply a complete fertilizer such as 13-13-13 to the soil at a low rate at least one week prior to planting the peas. Do not side-dress unless peas are showing signs of nutrient deficiency.

Insects of Concern

Aphids, worms, thrips, stinkbugs, leaf-footed bugs.

Diseases of Concern

Anthracnose, mosaic virus, several rots, rust, bacterial blight.

Harvest Time

Southern peas are generally harvested by the color of their pod, which differs depending on variety. For instance, if you pick a purple hull, the pod will be a dark purple when ready; other pod colors are green and slightly silver gray. The pods are generally the width of a pencil or slightly more slender when ready for harvest. The peas will be developed inside. Some gardeners harvest the pods early and treat them like snap beans. I prefer to hull the peas and eat without the pod. Harvest can occur as early as 70 days after seeding. As with all legume family crops, once harvest begins, be prepared to visit the garden every two to three days to harvest Southern peas.

A Brief Glance: Southern peas

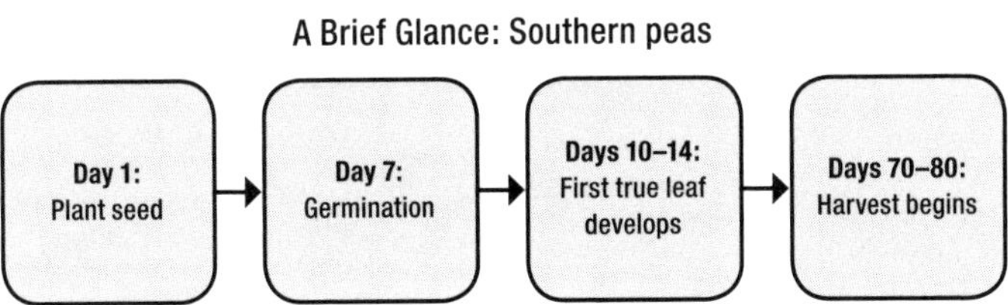

General Comments

After harvesting, shell quickly and store Southern peas in the refrigerator in ziplock bags or airtight containers. You can also blanch and freeze the peas.

I really enjoy growing Southern peas in the garden, especially the purple hull varieties. The purple pod color makes harvesting effortless; plus, it is a real standout in the garden. Looking to add a pop of color? Definitely plant these.

Did you know that LSU has a Southern pea breeding program? Popular varieties like Quickpick Pinkeye came from right here in our state!

Hydroponic towers in New Iberia community garden

Backyard garden of Joseph Landry, Bayou DuLarge

Home garden of C. J. Gueho, St. Gabriel (*Photo by Madeline Leblanc*)

Without raised beds providing adequate drainage, these vegetables would not survive.

Soaker hoses and drip tape are ideal watering systems to prevent excessive disease in smaller gardens.

Water within one hour of planting any vegetable.

Herbs and shallow-rooted vegetables such as lettuce mixes can be planted in small containers. Vertical height adds interest to a garden.

Some tomato varieties were bred for very small containers.

Add drainage to containers that were not originally intended for gardening.

Raised bed made of corrugated metal and wood at Almost Eden Nursery in DeRidder.

Decorate raised beds with paint, window planters, and colorful chickens to enhance the beauty of veggies.

Soil matters. Demonstration beds in Ascension Parish were used to test three soil types for vegetable growth.

Working rows by hand is hard. (*Photo by Dexter Fontenot*)

Preplant fertilizer is banded down the center of the row prior to planting seed or vegetable transplants.

A ladybug or ladybeetle walks amid a snack of whiteflies.

A tomato hornworm can strip an entire plant in a matter of days.

Leaf-footed bug on tomato

Aphids

Flea beetles

Cucumber beetle

Slug on a marigold. Watch for these in the early evening.

Thrip damage in shallots. Thrips are as tiny as dust, but their damage is large enough to see.

Whiteflies

To avoid burning the leaves, wash horticultural soap or liquid dish soap mixed with water off of plants 10–15 minutes after application.

Mulch between rows to prevent weeds.

Small seedlings should be labeled as many plants look similar when they first emerge from the soil.

Fairytale eggplant

Properly developed cucumber. The trellis helps prevent a yellow belly from developing and also makes spotting the fruit for harvest easier.

Even though one watermelon plant can take up ten feet, they can still be confined to raised beds and smaller garden spaces.

Thomas Laxton peas (*Photo by Erik Meyer*)

Pole beans require trellising.

Burgundy okra flower and pod

Asparagus ferns emerging in early spring

Lettuce comes in a variety of textures and colors.

Brussels sprouts developing on the stem

Yellow onions ready for harvest. Notice the foliage has fallen.

Shallots in a raised bed

Swiss chard

This basil has gone to seed. Strip the seeds off and save them in the refrigerator for next season or toss them back into the soil.

Trellising rosemary at Tuten Park in Lake Charles

Coriander (*Photo by Erik Meyer*)

Dill seed (*Photo by Erik Meyer*)

The author's vegetable garden

Family Malvaceae

OKRA

Planting Dates

Spring and summer okra

South Louisiana: April 1 through the end of June.

Central and North Louisiana: Starting April 1 (if soil is warm) or wait until mid-April and plant through the end of June.

Fall okra crop

Ratoon (cut back okra plants to knee height) in late summer. Doing so will continue production through the first freeze.

Plant Spacing

Space okra plants at least 12 inches apart. Single drill only.

Typical Number of Plants on a 10-Foot Row

8–10 okra plants.

Plant Spacing in a Container

Okra plants become quite large. Place 3 seeds in a 5-gallon container but thin emerging seedlings to 1–2 plants.

Typical Fertilizer Requirements

Okra needs relatively little fertilizer to produce heavy yields. If you excessively fertilized in the fall, apply no or a very low application of a complete fertilizer such as 13-13-13 to the soil of a raised bed or in-ground garden in the spring. Water in immediately. Do not side-dress okra unless the foliage does not appear healthy and green. Is your okra plant huge but not producing blooms? You've probably applied too much fertilizer. Start stressing the plant out to encourage blooms: reduce water (not to a wilting point), and take a stick and lightly knock the okra plants around. Wait a few days to see if blossoms set.

Insects of Concern

Aphids, fire ants, stinkbugs, leaf-footed bugs.

Diseases of Concern

Anthracnose.

Harvest Time

Harvest okra seed pods when they are 2–6 inches long to ensure that the okra is not tough. Some varieties like Cowhorn can be harvested when the pods are much longer, but most people prefer smaller, more tender pods. Cut off and throw extra-long pods in the compost pile, or allow them to dry to save seed for the following year. Once an okra flower has fully opened, it can take as little as three days before a pod is formed. When okra begins to produce, it is critical to harvest every other or every third day to pick optimum pods.

A Brief Glance: Okra

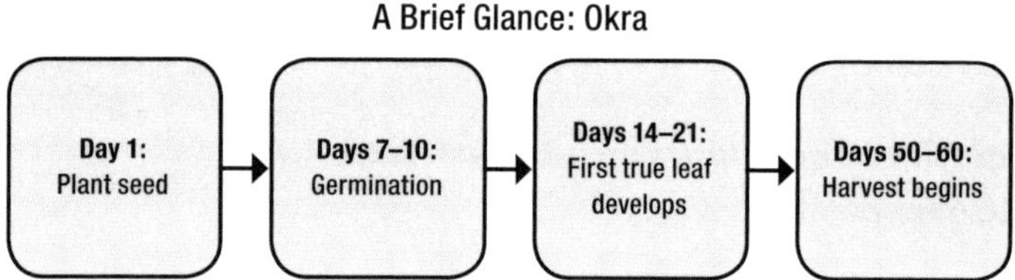

General Comments

Okra is an extremely easy crop to produce so long as you limit fertilizer. In the harvest section, I mention stressing the plant out if it isn't blooming. This practice may sound a bit odd, but it really does work for this crop! Don't try it on tomatoes . . . A plant does not have a brain, but it "knows" its main purpose in life is to reproduce. How do plants reproduce? By making seed. A little stress can manipulate the plant into "thinking" its life is almost over, so it starts to produce seed. Lightly knocking the plant with a stick does not mean breaking the plant; just give it a little hit.

Okra pods are typically light green or maroon. The maroon varieties are very pretty and can double as ornamental plants. In fact, I always tell novice vegetable gardeners if they like hibiscus flowers, they'll love okra flowers. They are in the same plant family, only smaller versions of their ornamental cousins. The maroon pods will lose some if not all of their color when cooked.

Do you notice fire ants near or on your okra plants? If so, look under the foliage. You'll also see aphids. Fire ants actually "farm" aphids. They like the sugary secretions that aphids release while feeding on okra foliage. Fire ants have been known to pick up aphids and bring them to the plants. This is a really neat symbiotic relationship, but if you don't enjoy sooty mold growing on okra because of the sugary secretions, an occasional bite from fire ants, and potentially poor-looking foliage (a huge aphid infestation would be needed for this to occur), then control the aphid population by applying a light horticultural oil (in cooler or cloudy weather only) or horticultural soap. Aphids reproduce as fast as every 7 days, so repeat applications (usually 2 to 3) of the insecticide of choice will be necessary to control the population.

Family Liliaceae

ASPARAGUS

Planting Dates

Note: Asparagus are typically planted from crowns (root balls with no foliage).

Spring asparagus crowns

South Louisiana: March 15 through May.

Central and North Louisiana: Beginning of April through end of May.

Plant Spacing

Space asparagus crowns on 12-inch centers. The roots of asparagus may touch, but the center point of the crown should be a foot from the next center. Single drill only.

Typical Number of Plants on a 10-Foot Row

10–12 asparagus plants.

Plant Spacing in a Container

A 5-gallon container can support one plant or crown; a 10-gallon container can support 3 crowns. After three years, thin the plants and separate crowns to avoid over-crowding roots and to allow the plants enough room to grow. Thinning may become an annual event in containers, especially smaller ones.

Typical Fertilizer Requirements

Asparagus is a heavy-feeding crop. It is also the only true perennial vegetable crop in Louisiana. Therefore, you should ensure your raised bed or garden row is built high with plenty of manure or compost or that a heavy dose of complete fertilizer such as 13-13-13 is incorporated into the soil prior to planting. Water in immediately. Once asparagus shoots emerge, fertilize again (side-dress) in March and repeat again mid-summer. Side-dress this perennial crop each spring with any fertilizer type but avoid manures. Manures should not be used as a side-dress right before you harvest the crop. Instead, add manures to the row in the summer. A general rule for all vegetable crops, no matter if they are annual or perennial, is to avoid applying fresh manures within 90 days of harvest. This is to reduce food safety concerns. Avoid fresh manures for side-dressing. After the first season is complete, fertilize asparagus annually at a heavy rate in early spring (March–April).

To side-dress one asparagus plant in a 5-gallon container, mix 1 tablespoon of a water-soluble 15% nitrogen fertilizer into a gallon of water. Pour the fertilizer solution into the container; avoid wetting the foliage. Use the entire gallon of solution per container. Apply this solution every spring and again midsummer or any time the crop turns a paler shade of green. Asparagus are heavy consumers of fertilizer.

Insects of Concern

None of significance. However, these plants are very large. Be on the lookout for bird nests and potentially rodents.

Diseases of Concern

None of significance.

A Brief Glance: Asparagus

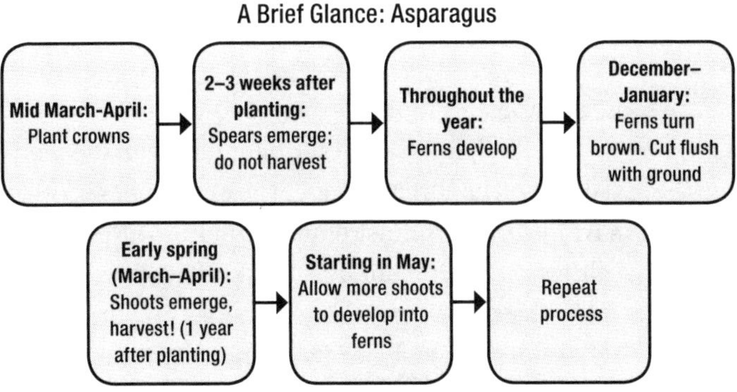

Harvest Time

Do not harvest asparagus in the same season in which it is first planted. Allow plants a full year in the garden before harvesting. After that first year of growth (March to March), you can harvest every year.

The second spring season, start harvesting asparagus shoots as they emerge from the soil. Continue to harvest for a month and a half or so, and then allow the shoots to develop into frond to capture enough sunlight and produce enough storage energy to continue this as a perennial crop in your garden.

Harvest asparagus shoots when they are 8 inches or shorter. Asparagus shoots can grow several inches in one day, so if you see questionable shoots in the morning, check them again that afternoon. They are probably already ready to be harvested.

General Comments

Because asparagus is a perennial vegetable crop, selecting its proper location in the garden is critical. This plant will remain in that same location for the next ten to fifteen years! The middle of the garden is probably not a good idea. On an edge, it won't interfere with seasonal tilling and replanting of other vegetable crops. Planting asparagus in a raised bed? Expect it to take over that bed in a few years. Be prepared for this very large crop (individual plants 6 feet tall by 5 feet wide) to consume a lot of space.

While asparagus is large, it will not produce huge quantities of spears the first few years. As the crowns mature, they increase yields slowly. This is a crop to be enjoyed by you and your family, not one that you will likely have enough to give to neighbors. That being said, after growing it, you will understand the high price commanded for it at the store.

Why are some asparagus shoots white and some green? The white shoots have been blanched; that is, the sunlight has been blocked from reaching them. To blanch asparagus, cover the emerging shoots in soil, protecting them from sunlight, thus reducing photosynthesis and the development of chlorophyll. Personally, I think short green shoots picked straight from the garden are so good, there's no purpose in blanching them . . . unless you just want a fun novelty item in your garden. Enjoy asparagus grilled or sautéed over a nice steak, piece of chicken, or grilled fish.

FALL AND WINTER VEGETABLES

Fall vegetable crops are those that can tolerate lower night-time temperatures and light frosts. Most fall vegetables can withstand a few hours of temperatures close to or at 32°F. If temperatures fall below 32°F, covering is recommended. If you are using light-colored, lightweight covers such as old sheets or weather-protection cloth, covers can remain on the plant through the day and up to a week. Dark-colored cloth will interfere with photosynthesis during the day and will surely affect plant growth. Using clear plastic materials can potentially burn the crop if a hot afternoon sun appears the next day.

To properly cover a crop, it is important to prevent air movement from going underneath the cloth, so secure the fabric to the ground with mulch, bricks, sandbags, or other heavy objects. I've even seen school gardens use heavy outdoor toys to keep frost protection over the garden. Simply covering the top portion of a plant and allowing the bottom portion to remain exposed is not helpful at all.

Fall crops that are a little more sensitive to frost and freezes include:

- Any crop that was planted late in the season and is a small seedling or has just emerged from the soil.
- Exposed flower heads (broccoli, cauliflower, and early developing artichoke bracts).
- Leaf lettuce (romaine, head lettuce, and butterhead types are more hardy than tender leaf lettuce types).

Other than frost and an occasional freeze, gardening in the fall is wonderful. We tend to have less disease and insect incidence, and except for a few really cold days, the weather is very pleasant. Also, most fall vegetable crops are leafy vegetables and require less sunlight than typical fruiting spring crops, so shadier yards can achieve better yields with fall crops. First-time vegetable gardeners should definitely attempt a fall crop or two.

Family Asteraceae

ARTICHOKES

Planting Dates

Note: It takes 10–12 weeks for a seed to develop into a seedling ready for transplant. To start your own artichokes from seed, purchase seed in July. Plant seeds only twice as deep as they are wide, no more than 1/4 to 1/2 inch. Seeds can be planted in any containers that are clean and have drainage holes. Keep seeds outdoors. A greenhouse or cold frame is too hot in Louisiana summer months to start seeds.

Fall artichokes

South Louisiana: Plant seedlings into the garden between late September and early November.

Central and North Louisiana: Plant seedlings into the garden between late September and the end of October.

Plant Spacing

Space artichoke plants at least 48 inches (4 feet) apart. Single drill only.

Typical Number of Plants on a 10-Foot Row

2 artichoke plants.

Plant Spacing in a Container

Mature artichokes are very large. Plant only one artichoke per container. Use a 7-gallon or larger container.

Typical Fertilizer Requirements

Artichokes are planted in the fall but won't be ready to harvest until the spring. Technically, artichokes are perennial, but Louisiana's hot, humid, disease-prone summers can affect plant health so much that most gardeners treat them as an annual crop. Prolonged time needed to harvest combined with the fact that these are massive plants (at least 4 feet by 4 feet) makes fertilizing a must for proper growth and to achieve acceptable yields.

In raised beds and in-ground gardens, apply a complete fertilizer such as 13-13-13 to the soil at a heavy rate one to three weeks prior to planting. Water in immediately. Build rows high or dedicate a large space in the raised bed to this plant. Adding manures and organic matter is strongly encouraged to help feed this plant through the winter months. Side-dress artichoke plants in the early spring (late February–early March) and again right after your first harvest. At each side-dressing, apply 1–2 teaspoons of a 15% nitrogen fertilizer per plant.

To side-dress one artichoke in a 7-gallon container, mix 1 tablespoon of a water-soluble 15% nitrogen fertilizer into a gallon of water. Pour the fertilizer solution into the container; avoid wetting the foliage. One gallon of solution is plenty of fertilizer to use per side-dress application. If the container is extremely wet, break this application into 2 applications 3–4 days apart.

Insects of Concern

Aphids, flea beetles, worms, loopers.

Diseases of Concern

Gray mold (in very rainy periods), bacterial crown rot.

Harvest Time

Harvest artichoke buds before they open. The bracts will be tight and approximately 3–4 inches in diameter. Artichoke are in the same plant family as thistle, so expect lovely, purple thistle-like flowers if you missed peak harvest. The more you harvest, the more new flowers buds will develop, similar to deadheading daisies and other ornamental flowering plants. The buds develop at the top of a stem or stalk. I always cut the stalk at least midway back and then remove the head to bring inside. A typical plant can support 10 to 15 buds at one time. The larger buds develop first. Later in the spring, buds become smaller but remain tasty.

A Brief Glance: Artichokes

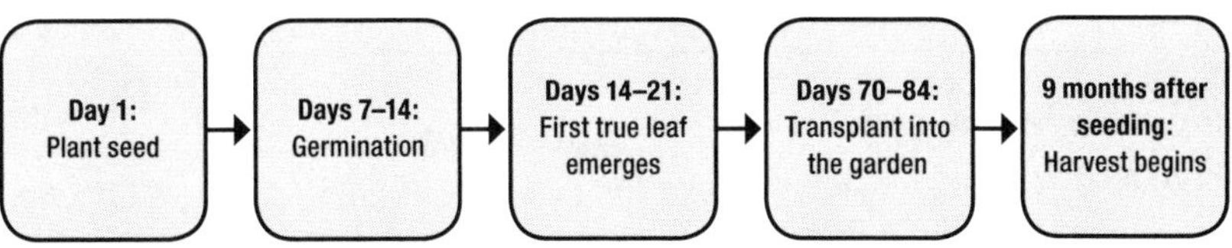

General Comments

Artichokes are huge plants, the dinosaurs of the garden. Spacing them properly is essential to meet their growth and development needs as well as to achieve acceptable harvests. Because these massive plants will be in the garden for most of the year, plan accordingly. You'll probably want to place them on the edge of the garden, similar to asparagus.

Artichokes need a lot of water to grow and thrive, but at the same time they will not tolerate saturated soils. Consider installing a drip hose for this crop and setting a timer to ensure you are watering regularly—especially if you plan on being out of town often. Apply a heavy layer of mulch around the base of seedlings to help maintain soil moisture, reduce weeds, and give an added layer of protection to the roots during the winter months.

If a frost or light freeze occurs and ice forms on the foliage, avoid trying to break it off. Simply water the base of the plant and let the sun naturally melt away the ice. If temperatures are expected to go below 32°F for several hours or more, covering is helpful. A lightweight white or light-colored sheet will work just fine, or you can invest in weather- or frost-protection cloth offered at most hardware stores.

Technically, you are eating the flower of this crop. If you happen to miss a few buds, simply place them in a vase; you haven't lost anything. They make wonderful cut flowers lasting almost two weeks. Want longer color? Cut them and hang them upside down to dry for year-round color that can be added to wreaths, bouquets, and other decorative items. But try not to let too many go to flower, because this is a veggie garden!

LETTUCE

Planting Dates

Fall lettuce

South Louisiana: Plant seedlings into the garden between late August and early November.

Central and North Louisiana: Plant seedlings into the garden between mid-August and the end of October.

Early spring lettuce

Plant seedlings into the garden between mid-January and the end of February.

Plant Spacing

Space head, butterhead, and large-leaf lettuce transplants 12 inches apart on a double-drilled row. Leaf lettuce and some lettuce mixes can also be direct seeded into the garden. If direct seeding, thin plants to 2–4 inches apart for optimum growth.

Typical Number of Plants on a 10-Foot Row

18–20 transplants on a double-drilled row.

Plant Spacing in a Container

Lettuce spacing in a container depends on type of lettuce and size of the container. Three head lettuce plants, 3 romaine lettuce plants, 6 leaf lettuce plants, or 2 butterhead lettuce plants will fit nicely in a 5-gallon container. Lettuce is a shallow-rooted crop. It is more important that containers be wide than deep. I've even planted lettuce directly into potting-soil bags. When direct seeding leaf lettuce in a container, simply sprinkle the seeds on top of the soil and gently rake them into the soil with your fingertips, to not bury them too deep. After the seeds emerge and have their first true leaf, thin the plants to allow at least 4 inches between leaf lettuce plants. Use transplants if growing head, romaine, or butterhead types in containers.

Typical Fertilizer Requirements

Incorporate a preplant application of fertilizer into the soil a week or two prior to transplanting or direct seeding a lettuce crop. A medium rate of a complete fertilizer such as 13-13-13 is generally adequate for raised beds and in-ground gardens. Water in immediately. Side-dress lettuce two weeks after planting and again three weeks later. At each side-dressing, apply 1–2 teaspoons of a 15% nitrogen fertilizer per plant. Water in immediately.

To side-dress lettuce in a 5-gallon container, mix 1 tablespoon of a water-soluble 15% nitrogen fertilizer into a gallon of water. Pour the fertilizer solution into the container; avoid wetting the foliage. One gallon of solution is plenty of fertilizer to use per side-dress application. If the container is extremely wet, break this application into 2 applications 3–4 days apart.

If direct seeding or transplanting leaf lettuce, side-dress again immediately after the first harvest to encourage foliage to flush again.

Insects of Concern

Aphids, flea beetles, worms and loopers, snails, slugs.

Diseases of Concern

Diseases in lettuce are not all that common in Louisiana. Damping off (a rotting of the base of the plant) can occur early on if you are using contaminated potting soil to start seedlings or if your garden soil is over-saturated. Fix drainage problems for optimum growth.

Harvest Time

There are literally hundreds of varieties of lettuce available for home gardeners to grow. Romaine, leaf, and butterhead perform the best in comparison to head (including iceberg) types. Each type of lettuce will be harvested at a different time, but start looking for the crop to peak around 55 days after planting. Lettuce texture, leaf color, and plant height and width also greatly vary by variety and type. In general, look for a full, uniformly developed head that has not bolted (gone to flower). Once a lettuce plant has bolted, the flavor becomes extremely bitter. If you cut a lettuce head near the base of the stem, you'll also notice milky-colored latex that emerges from the stem. The more latex present, the older the lettuce and the more likely it is to taste bitter.

A Brief Glance: Lettuce

General Comments

If you've only consumed the typical light green ball of iceberg-type lettuce, it is time to expand your palate. Lettuces range in color from pale green to lime green, to variegated with spots and stripes of reds and greens, to dark purples and bright reds. Mixing up varieties will also add color to a rather "green" garden in the fall. Dots of bright red and purple will surely attract visitors' attention, and you'll be providing tours of the garden as much as your new bathroom remodel.

While many gardeners direct seed lettuce, I prefer planting transplants. Direct-seed lettuce crops are hard to manage for weeds and are usually crowded. Many seed companies add romaine and butterhead types to leaf lettuce mixes, so you end up with smaller, non-uniform heads. Direct seeding is a good choice if planting leaf types into containers, but in raised beds and in-ground gardens, I recommend transplanting. Planting each seedling on a 12-inch center will help you achieve a round, full, uniform head of lettuce.

If you decide to start seed to grow your own transplants or to direct seed into the ground, note that small plants will develop in about 5 weeks. Germinating lettuce seed can be difficult. Read the packet carefully. Many lettuce varieties require sunlight for germination. This means you should press the seed into the soil only two times as deep as it is wide. Some gardeners invest in a small bag of vermiculite and shake a thin layer over the soil to allow light but keep the seed from running all over the garden space after watering it. Vermiculite is mined from the earth in combination with other minerals. When heated, it puffs or expands. It is used in many industries but commonly in horticulture for seed germination or as an additive to germinating mixes to allow for better soil porosity.

When harvesting leaf lettuce, you can leave 2–3 inches of foliage attached to the roots, side-dress, water, and allow the plant to flush out again for a second and sometimes third harvest if you plant early in the season. Head and romaine types will not flush out again. Some gardeners harvest the entire lettuce plant, with roots. They claim that immediately washing soil off the roots and storing the lettuce with root ball attached prevents the lettuce from dehydrating quickly when stored in the refrigerator. Lettuce should be kept cool. If the foliage goes limp before it is consumed, submerge the head of lettuce in a clean bucket of water. It will rehydrate. Try to consume all harvested lettuce within about three days. Successional plantings are very helpful if you don't eat lettuce daily.

Mulching is necessary with lettuce crops. If you do not mulch, you are sure to taste grit in your salad, even if you have thoroughly cleaned the lettuce.

This crop is extremely easy to grow and one that novice gardeners should plant!

Family Brassicaceae

Brassica plants include broccoli, cabbage, cauliflower, mustard greens, collard greens, and Brussels sprouts. This vegetable group is often referred to as "cole crops." The cooking smell of these crops often has a sulfur-like odor. To prevent this odor from becoming stronger, avoid using ammonium sulfate as a side-dress fertilizer. People frequently ask if broccoli and cauliflower foliage is edible. Yes, it is. But most people prefer the taste of mustard, cabbage, collards, and turnip greens, which are tenderer. There is a vast amount of foliage that goes uneaten with these crops. Don't hesitate to add it to your compost pile. Why not take advantage of that great nitrogen source for future crops?

BROCCOLI

Planting Dates

Fall broccoli

Plant transplants into the garden late August through early November. You may plant through late November if freezes are not expected for the first month or you are willing to cover plants while they are young and tender.

Early spring broccoli

Plant transplants into the garden mid-January through late February.

Plant Spacing

Space broccoli plants 12–18 inches apart. Double drilling is fine.

Typical Number of Plants on a 10-Foot Row

13–20 broccoli plants per double-drilled row.

Plant Spacing in a Container

Plant 1–3 broccoli plants per 5-gallon container. Note that the more broccoli plants are placed in a container, the smaller the head size.

Typical Fertilizer Requirements

In raised beds and in-ground gardens, apply a complete fertilizer such as 13-13-13 to the soil at a medium rate one to three weeks prior to planting. Water in immediately. Side-dress broccoli two weeks after planting and again three weeks later. I also side-dress broccoli immediately after I cut off the main head. This helps increase the size of side shoots. At each side-dressing, apply one teaspoon of a 15% nitrogen fertilizer per plant.

To side-dress broccoli in a 5-gallon container, mix 1 tablespoon of a water-soluble 15% nitrogen fertilizer into a gallon of water. Pour the fertilizer solution into the container; avoid wetting the foliage. One gallon of solution is plenty of fertilizer to use per side-dress application. If the container is extremely wet, break this application into 2 applications 3–4 days apart.

Insects of Concern

Aphids, worms, loopers.

Diseases of Concern

Black rot, soft rot, downy mildew.

Harvest Time

Broccoli heads are typically harvested before they have opened up into yellow flowers. A tight bud is preferred, although I've been told by some food critics that a slightly larger bud with some yellow showing is very flavorful. Depending on which variety you select, the color of the plants will be green to blue. Main head sizes range from 3 to 10 or more inches in diameter.

If you plant broccoli raab, also known as broccoli rabe or broccoli rapini, a related plant, both the foliage and heads are consumed. Cut and prepare foliage as you would mustard greens. Heads will flower very quickly, so harvesting every other day is necessary. Otherwise, you'll have an amazing show of yellow blooms. Head size is typically very small, 1–3 inches in diameter, and it appears as if the plant is only producing side shoots.

A Brief Glance: Broccoli

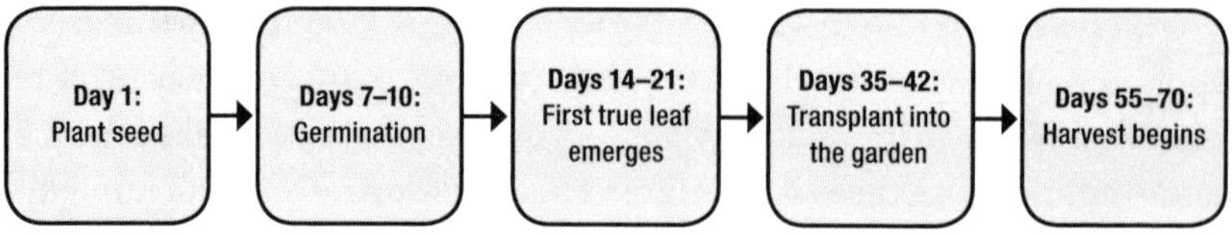

Day 1: Plant seed	→	Days 7–10: Germination	→	Days 14–21: First true leaf emerges	→	Days 35–42: Transplant into the garden	→	Days 55–70: Harvest begins

General Comments

Broccoli is a great crop for a small garden, because it just keeps producing! If you carefully cut the stem of the main head short (no longer than 5 inches) and side-dress immediately, it will produce prolific side shoots for months to come.

To prolong the post-harvest life of broccoli, store it in cooler temperatures.

Allowing broccoli to go to seed makes a beautiful show of yellow flowers. I don't recommend this early in the season, because your first priority in the vegetable garden is to produce something to eat. Beauty is often associated with growing vegetables, but purposely allowing something to flower isn't what we are trying to achieve. However, later in the season, when you've had your fill of this crop, allow it to go to flower. One of my favorite garden compliments is, "What is that yellow blossom?"... My reply, "Broccoli plants." The blossoms attract more than human spectators, too; they are wonderful for attracting pollinators. It is nice to let the bees know where your garden is located, in case they'd like to revisit in the spring when the cucumbers and other cucurbits are planted!

I definitely recommend that novice gardeners try growing this crop. You'll be amazed at the rapid growth, beautiful plant foliage, and general popularity as a side dish (notwithstanding the taste of a certain past president). It requires less sunlight than most spring crops and, with the exception of controlling a few worms, is easy to maintain.

BRUSSELS SPROUTS

Planting Dates

Late August through early November.

Plant Spacing

Space Brussels sprout plants 18–24 inches apart.

Typical Number of Plants on a 10-Foot Row

7–8 Brussels sprout plants.

Plant Spacing in a Container

Plant 1–2 Brussels sprout plants per 5-gallon container.

Typical Fertilizer Requirements

In raised beds and in-ground gardens, apply a complete fertilizer such as 13-13-13 to the soil at a heavy rate one to three weeks prior to planting. Water in immediately. Side-dress Brussels sprouts two weeks after planting and again three weeks later. I also side-dress the plants in the early spring (late January–March) because they take so long to produce. At each side-dressing, apply one teaspoon of a 15% nitrogen fertilizer per plant.

To side-dress Brussels sprouts in a 5-gallon container, mix 1 tablespoon of a water-soluble 15% nitrogen fertilizer into a gallon of water. Pour the fertilizer solution into the container; avoid wetting the foliage. One gallon of solution is plenty of fertilizer to use per side-dress application. If the container is extremely wet, break this application into 2 applications 3–4 days apart.

Insects of Concern

Aphids, worms and loopers, snails, slugs, flea beetles.

Diseases of Concern

Bacterial leaf spot, downy mildew, powdery mildew, several rots.

Harvest Time

Brussels sprouts can be individually harvested or the entire stalk can be harvested at one time. Sprouts develop first at the base of the plant and continue upward along the stem. The sprouts are not ready to be harvested until they are approximately 1–2 inches in diameter and firm. You can remove lower sprouts and older yellow foliage or wait until the entire stem is ready to be cut. Some gardeners will cut off newly developed foliage in the spring and then harvest a week or more later. Harvest usually occurs in Louisiana in the early to mid-spring. Patience is a must for this crop!

A Brief Glance: Brussels sprouts

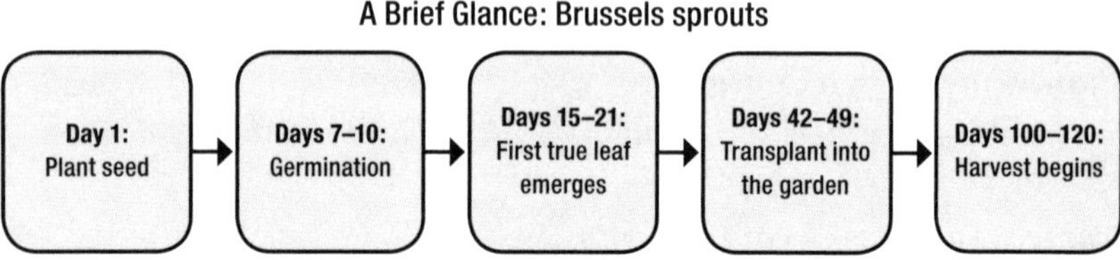

General Comments

Brussels sprouts need at least six hours of sunlight each day for optimum yields and growth. Avoid planting in shady areas of the garden. And these giant plants will be in the garden for a while, so give some thought to their location. The middle of the garden is not ideal if you are also planting early spring crops. Although Brussels sprout plants are very large, they are quite suited to growing in containers and raised beds. They prefer middle to higher soil pH for optimum growth and also to limit some plant disease.

This is a fun plant to grow; children love looking at the "mini cabbages" all along the stem. Try at least a few plants in the garden once before declaring you don't like the taste!

CABBAGE

Planting Dates

Fall cabbage

South Louisiana: Late August through early December.

Central and North Louisiana: Late August through early November. Cabbage plants are very hardy and can withstand cooler temperatures than other crops.

Early spring cabbage

Plant transplants into the garden starting in mid-January through late February.

Plant Spacing

Space cabbage plants 9–12 inches apart for smaller heads and up to 18 inches apart for larger heads. Think about how much cabbage you can eat at one time and space accordingly. Double drilling is fine.

Typical Number of Plants on a 10-Foot Row

13–20 cabbage seedlings in a double-drilled row.

Plant Spacing in a Container

Plant 1–3 cabbage plants per 5-gallon container. Note that head size will be smaller the more cabbage plants are placed in a container.

Typical Fertilizer Requirements

In raised beds and in-ground gardens, apply a complete fertilizer such as 13-13-13 to the soil at a medium rate one to three weeks prior to planting. Water in immediately. Side-dress cabbage two weeks after planting and again three weeks later. At each side-dressing, apply one teaspoon of a 15% nitrogen fertilizer per plant.

To side-dress cabbage in a 5-gallon container, mix 1 tablespoon of a water-soluble 15% nitrogen fertilizer into a gallon of water. Pour the fertilizer solution into the container; avoid wetting the foliage. One gallon of solution is plenty of fertilizer to use per side-dress application. If the container is extremely wet, break this application into 2 applications 3–4 days apart.

Insects of Concern

Aphids, worms, loopers.

Diseases of Concern

Various rots, Fusarium wilt, damping off.

Harvest Time

Cabbage heads are ready to be harvested when you push the top of the head (or ball) and it feels similar to a softball. If you can feel air space or hear a crunching noise when you push on the top of the head, it is not fully developed. You can eat it, but you will get more out of the crop if you allow it to develop a little longer. An exception to this rule is cone-shaped head cabbages such as Caraflex, which will not feel as hard as a softball. Cabbage is over-mature when the head has cracked.

A Brief Glance: Cabbage

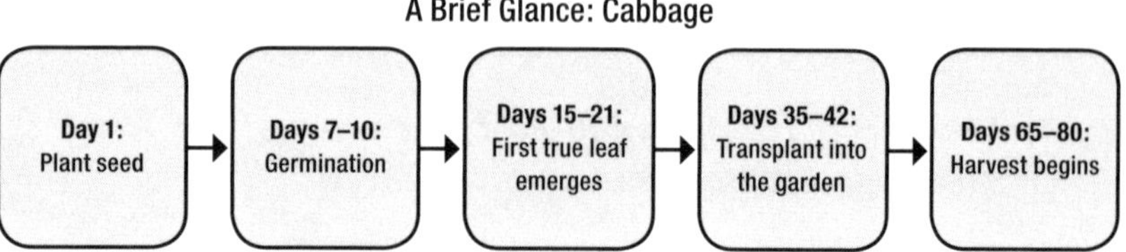

General Comments

Cabbage is another beautiful crop and definitely one worth planting in the garden, even if you have only one container. If you have to forgo planting annual fall color at your front door, cabbage is a great alternative. The only down side to cabbage is that once you've harvested it, that's it. Sometimes small balls form at the base of foliage left in the garden after the main head is cut. There is no need to try applying more fertilizer at this point; they will not develop into small or large heads, but instead remain the size of Brussels sprouts.

The peskiest part of growing cabbage is scouting really early in the season for worms and loopers. If you see these little guys, pinch them off or spray. They like to get into the cabbage head while it is young and loose. Not controlling these pests early in the season will result in a perfectly developed cabbage head you are very proud of until you bring it inside and chop into it. You'll notice many tunnels drilled throughout the head—sure to turn you off from preparing your homemade coleslaw, cabbage rolls, and egg rolls. Partner this crop with carrots, and start trying all kinds of new recipes!

CAULIFLOWER

Planting Dates

Fall cauliflower

Late August through early November. Planting through late November is acceptable if freezes are not expected for the first month or you are willing to cover plants while they are young and tender.

Early spring cauliflower

Plant transplants into the garden mid-January through late February.

Plant Spacing

Space cauliflower plants 12–18 inches apart. Single drill only. These are large plants.

Typical Number of Plants on a 10-Foot Row

7–10 cauliflower plants.

Plant Spacing in a Container

Plant one cauliflower plant per 5-gallon container. If you want more than one, use a 10-gallon or larger container.

Typical Fertilizer Requirements

In raised beds and in-ground gardens, apply a complete fertilizer such as 13-13-13 to the soil at a medium rate one to three weeks prior to planting. Water in immediately. Side-dress cauliflower two weeks after planting and again three weeks later. At each side-dressing, apply one teaspoon of a 15% nitrogen fertilizer per plant.

To side-dress one cauliflower plant in a 5-gallon container, mix 1 tablespoon of a water-soluble 15% nitrogen fertilizer into a gallon of water. Pour the fertilizer solution into the container; avoid wetting the foliage. One gallon of solution is plenty of fertilizer to use per side-dress application. If the container is extremely wet, break this application into 2 applications 3–4 days apart.

Insects of Concern

Aphids, worms, loopers.

Diseases of Concern

Damping off, downy mildew, several rots.

Harvest Time

Cauliflower heads are typically harvested while they are firm and before the individual florets are distinguishable from one another.

Depending on the variety and how well you manage the crop, typical head size ranges from 4 to 8 inches in diameter. Cauliflower does not make side shoots. You will only harvest one main head from each plant.

A Brief Glance: Cauliflower

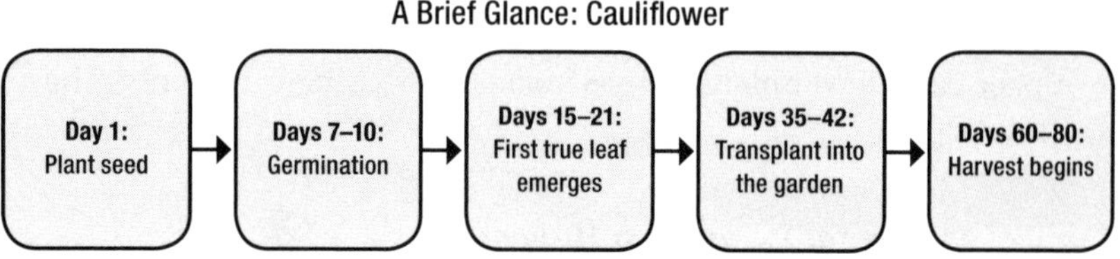

General Comments

Cauliflower heads are very susceptible to excessive sunlight. If foliage has an open form and is not upright and covering the newly developing head, you'll need to take action. Either cut off a bottom older leaf and wrap it over the developing head or bear-hug all of the foliage together and loosely tie it with a piece of string or twine. This will allow the plant to continue to grow but protect the head from sunlight. This process is termed "blanching."

Sunlight will cause white cauliflower heads to turn a pale yellow. The flower bud is still edible, but most people do not like the look of it. Also, exposed heads will turn a light shade of lavender in frosts or freezes. This color is definitely not attractive to consumers.

Besides the typical white cauliflower heads, several varieties boast colorful heads. One mixture of seeds called "Colored Mix" features a combination of lime green, soft orange, and dark purple heads. Other colorful varieties that perform well in Louisiana include Graffiti, which is LSU purple in color, and Cheddar, which is dark orange. The colorful heads do not need to be blanched, but beware: if you plan on steaming or cooking them, they will lose a lot of their color in the water.

KALE

Planting Dates

Fall kale

Kale transplants can be planted into the garden late August through early November.

If direct seeding, complete all seeding prior to mid-October.

Early spring kale

Plant transplants into the garden from mid-January through late February.

Plant Spacing

Space kale plants 6–18 inches apart. Double drilling is fine. If direct seeding, thin plants when they are very small to about 3 inches apart and then thin again once foliage has reached 5 inches tall to 12 inches apart for optimum growth.

Typical Number of Plants on a 10-Foot Row

15–20 kale plants per double-drilled row.

Plant Spacing in a Container

Kale comes in a number of varieties, some with flat leaves and some with curly. Mature heights and widths also vary. Are you planting dinosaur or lacinato kale? Limit to 1–2 plants per 5-gallon container. Upwards of five plants of smaller, compact varieties can grow in a 5-gallon container.

Typical Fertilizer Requirements

In raised beds and in-ground gardens, apply a complete fertilizer such as 13-13-13 to the soil at a medium rate one to three weeks prior to planting. Water in immediately. Side-dress kale two weeks after planting and again three weeks later. At each side-dressing, apply one teaspoon of a 15% nitrogen fertilizer per plant.

To side-dress kale in a 5-gallon container, mix 1 tablespoon of a water-soluble 15% nitrogen fertilizer into a gallon of water. Pour the fertilizer solution into the container; avoid wetting the foliage. One gallon of solution is plenty of fertilizer to use per side-dress application. If the container is extremely wet, break this application into 2 applications 3–4 days apart.

Insects of Concern

Aphids, worms, loopers.

Diseases of Concern

Very few in Louisiana.

Harvest Time

Kale is typically harvested 55–75 days after planting into the garden, or later if direct seeded. Many gardeners harvest the outer leaves of the plant when they have reached 8–10 inches high. If desired, you can harvest the entire plant while allowing 2–3 inches of foliage to remain attached to the roots. Side-dress and water immediately after a harvest like this. The kale will flush again in a few weeks. Similar to lettuce, as temperatures warm and as the plant ages, kale will develop a bitter taste. Juvenile foliage is much more pleasing.

A Brief Glance: Kale

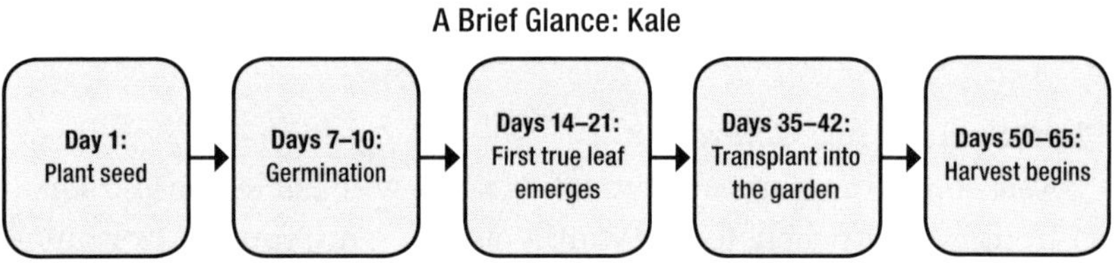

General Comments

When purchasing kale transplants at hardware stores and plant nurseries, look for edible varieties. The ornamental varieties, while pretty and theoretically fit for consumption, are tougher and less flavorful than their edible counterparts.

Kale comes in many sizes and foliage textures. This leafy vegetable prefers moist but not saturated soils, so pay particular attention to how well your garden retains moisture. Using soaker hoses will greatly increase growth.

Try kale raw in salads, baked into chips, and added to smoothies. This is one vegetable Popeye would have liked to get his hands on!

MUSTARD, COLLARD, & TURNIP GREENS

Planting Dates

Fall greens

Directly seed into the garden late August through early November.

Early spring greens

Directly seed into the garden mid-January through March.

Note: Mustard greens that are heat-set can actually be planted from July throughout most of the year. Avoid December. (Heat-set varieties of vegetables are those that breeders note as having tolerance to high day- and nighttime temperatures. They are simply hybrids, not GMOs.)

Plant Spacing

To achieve even stands of directly seeded greens, either mix seeds with some sand in your hand and gently spread down the row, or place seeds in an old spice container and shake as you walk down the row. It is critical to plant seeds only twice as deep as they are wide—1/8 to 1/4 inch deep at max. Greens are typically thinned after they have developed their first true leaf. Thin mustard and collard plants to 2–3 inches between plants, and thin turnip greens to 3–6 inches between plants. Use the larger 6-inch spacing if you prefer to harvest and eat larger roots.

Typical Number of Plants on a 10-Foot Row

So little seed is needed for a 10-foot row that it is hard to estimate the quantity you'll need. One pack is plenty as 1/8 ounce usually covers 100 feet.

Plant Spacing in a Container

Scatter seeds into the top 1/4 inch of the container. Thin plants after they have developed their first true leaf. Thin to 2–6 inches between plants.

Typical Fertilizer Requirements

In raised beds and in-ground gardens, apply a complete fertilizer such as 13-13-13 to the soil at a medium rate one to three weeks prior to planting. Water in immediately. Make sure the fertilizer is banded 4 inches below the soil line or, if broadcast in, wait at least one week prior to planting seeds. Side-dress greens two weeks after planting and again three weeks later. I also side-dress greens immediately after the first and sometimes second harvest to encourage faster regrowth. At each side-dressing, apply one teaspoon of a 15% nitrogen fertilizer every 8 to 10 inches down the row.

To side-dress greens in a 5-gallon container, mix 1 tablespoon of a water-soluble 15% nitrogen fertilizer into a gallon of water. Pour the fertilizer solution into the container; avoid wetting the foliage. One gallon of solution is plenty of fertilizer to use per side-dress application. If the container is extremely wet, break this application into 2 applications 3–4 days apart.

Insects of Concern

Aphids, worms and loopers, flea beetles, snails, slugs.

Diseases of Concern

Anthracnose, bacterial leaf spot, downy mildew.

Harvest Time

Mustard greens are tender and usually 4–18 inches tall when harvested. Collard greens are 6–18 inches tall when harvested and have a firmer texture than mustard greens. Both plants will become very bushy. Many gardeners remove the outer foliage and allow the plant to continue producing leaves, slowly removing foliage as the plant grows. I prefer to cut the entire plant back to about 2–3 inches from the ground and side-dress it, allowing it to grow again. To avoid having all of your greens ready to harvest at the same time, consider successional plantings. But remember that you need a lot of foliage to "make a mess" of greens, as they are mostly comprised of water and will quickly reduce when cooked down.

A Brief Glance: Mustards, Collard, and Turnip Greens

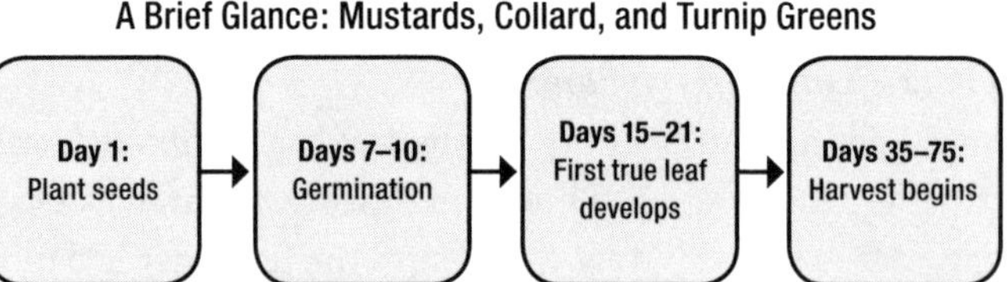

General Comments

Greens are a super-easy crop to grow, pending two things:

- Do not plant seeds too deep. They will not emerge from the soil. If they do germinate, emergence will be very spotty and you will be discouraged. Only plant seeds twice as deep as they are wide. Look how tiny these seeds are—for $2 or less, you probably purchased 1,000 seeds. Pressing them into the soil and then lightly watering in will help you avoid planting them too deep.
- If your garden soil has a lot of clay, it has the potential of forming a crust after being watered. It is difficult for newly emerging seedlings to penetrate this hard crust. Knowing your soil type will help you decide how to plant the seeds. In heavier clay soils, I press my seeds into the ground and then *very lightly* cover the seeds with a loose potting soil and water in. This practice will prevent the soil from crusting and encourage much better germination.

With a little insect control and proper thinning of plants, you're sure to be successful with this crop! Don't stress over thinning plants; simply wait until the foliage has started to broaden and rip out plants every few inches. Throw these away—they will not transplant well.

RADISHES & TURNIPS

Radish Planting Dates

Fall radishes

Direct seed radish into the garden September through early November.

Early spring radishes

Direct seed radish into the garden January through late March.

Turnip Planting Dates

Turnips may be direct seeded into the garden from August all the way through late February.

Plant Spacing

Space radish seed 1–2 inches apart and turnip seed 2–6 inches apart. It is not necessary to plant the seed in rows; broadcasting the seed over a raised bed or container is fine.If direct seeding, thin plants when they are very small to about 3 inches apart, and then thin again once foliage has reached about 5 inches tall to 12 inches apart for optimum growth. Plant the seed of both root crops no deeper than 1/8 inch.

Typical Number of Plants on a 10-Foot Row

You can plant up to three rows on a 4-foot-wide bed/row. So you will have 150–300 radish plants or 60–150 turnip plants per 10-foot row.

Plant Spacing in a Container

Sprinkle radish or turnip seeds over the soil surface of the container. Gently rake in seed with your fingertips. Thin radish seed to one inch between plants and turnip seed to 3–6 inches between plants depending on how large you like the root crop.

Typical Fertilizer Requirements

In raised beds and in-ground gardens, apply a complete fertilizer such as 13-13-13 to the soil at a medium rate one to three weeks prior to planting. Water in immediately. Side-dress these root crops three weeks after planting and again three weeks later. At each side-dressing, apply one teaspoon of a 15% nitrogen fertilizer every 8–10 inches down the side of the row.

To side-dress radish or turnip in a 5-gallon container, mix 1 tablespoon of a water-soluble 15% nitrogen fertilizer into a gallon of water. Pour the fertilizer solution into the container; avoid wetting the foliage. One gallon of solution is plenty of fertilizer to use per side-dress application. If the container is extremely wet, break this application into 2 applications 3–4 days apart.

Note: If the weather is very cold and the crops are not at least 3 inches high after three weeks, wait until they have reached this height before side-dressing.

Insects of Concern

Aphids, flea beetles, worms, loopers.

Diseases of Concern

Fusarium wilt, downy mildew, scab.

Harvest Time

Radishes are typically harvested 25–30 days after direct seeding into the garden. Turnips require a little more time, needing 40–50 days before harvest. In both cases, you will see the top of the root sticking slightly above the soil line. A recent trend is to harvest turnips when they are the size of a silver dollar. Small turnips have a milder, more delicate flavor. Early harvest will greatly reduce disease and insect pressure because you are cutting down on the number of days spent in the garden. But it will also affect your yield of turnip greens. While most people think of these as root crops, the tops or foliage of both radishes and turnips can be consumed. Turnip greens are usually cooked, while radish greens are eaten raw and mixed with other greens in salads.

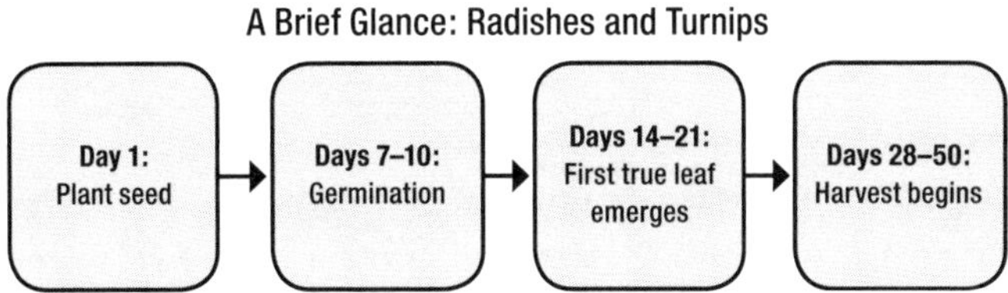

General Comments

Looking for a fast crop to grow with young children? Try turnips and radishes. Both are easily planted and harvested within the school year and may be just the crop to start these young, energetic, but less than patient minds growing because they will see results very quickly.

Sauté or panfry either of these root crops with a variety of other vegetables, or simply eat radishes raw in salads.

If you are only interested in eating the root portion of this crop and insects are feeding on the foliage, reduce the amount of insecticides you spray. Unless the foliage is severely damaged by insects (more than 50% eliminated), the root will still develop.

Alliums

Alliums are vegetables prized primarily for their ability to flavor other foods. Many gardeners claim that using these crops, especially garlic, in between other vegetable crops will ward off insects because of the intense smell. While there is great merit in companion plantings of vegetables, herbs, and flowers for increased pollination, several garlic plants will not ward off mass infestations of insects. Neat fact: *Allium* is the Latin word for garlic.

GARLIC

Planting Dates

Plant toes (the broken-up cloves) mid-September through the end of November.

Plant Spacing

Space garlic toes point side up roughly 4–6 inches apart and 1 inch deep. If the soil is well prepared, you will not need a trowel or other garden tool; simply shove the bulb into the soil. Garlic toes can be planted randomly across raised beds, scattered in a container, or in rows. If you are planting in rows, allow at least 6 inches between rows in a larger bed.

Typical Number of Plants on a 10-Foot Row

60–90 garlic bulbs.

Plant Spacing in a Container

Plant up to 8 toes of garlic per 5-gallon container.

Typical Fertilizer Requirements

In raised beds and in-ground gardens, apply a complete fertilizer such as 13-13-13 to the soil at a heavy rate one to three weeks prior to planting. Water in immediately. Side-dress garlic monthly through harvest. At each side-dressing, apply 2 teaspoons of a 15% nitrogen fertilizer every 8–10 inches down the row.

To side-dress garlic in a 5-gallon container, mix 1/2 tablespoon of a water-soluble 15% nitrogen fertilizer into a gallon of water. Pour the fertilizer solution into the container; avoid wetting the foliage. One gallon of solution is plenty of fertilizer to use per side-dress application. If the container is extremely wet, break this application into 2 applications 3–4 days apart.

Insects of Concern

Thrips.

Diseases of Concern

Downy mildew.

Harvest Time

Harvest garlic when 50% or more of the foliage has turned yellow or fallen over. This typically occurs 200 days after planting. Do not pull cloves up immediately. Break the roots from the soil by using a pitchfork or shovel and simply cutting roots below the soil line. After several days to a week, pull cloves from the soil. Dry bulbs in a dark or covered outdoor area with a fan blowing on them constantly for about a week. Cut tops from bulbs 1/2–1 inch above the clove. Or braid the tops to create beautiful garlic wreaths.

A Brief Glance: Garlic

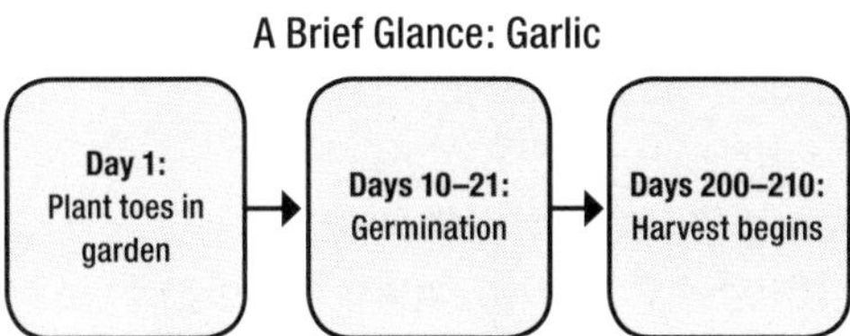

General Comments

Garlic is fun to grow, but like most alliums, you must be patient with it. These crops require a long time before they are ready for harvest, generally nine months.

Weeds can be difficult to control. Carefully hand remove or hoe to avoid chopping off smaller plants at the soil line. Herbicides with the active ingredient sethoxydim greatly reduce the amount of winter grass weeds between garlic rows. Apply heavy layers of mulch to avoid big weed infestations.

If tops start turning yellow and dying out too early in the season, do not assume that your garlic has matured at a rapid rate and is ready for harvesting. This is probably an indication that you are not applying enough fertilizer. Get some nitrogen on them fast. Apply 1/2 cup of 13-13-13 per 10-foot row or a teaspoon of calcium nitrate every foot to remedy the situation.

ONIONS

Planting Dates

Direct seed onions into small trays or broadcast seed into several pots for later in-ground planting mid-September to mid-October.

Transplant the seedlings—called "sets"—into the garden December through January.

Plant Spacing

When the onion sets are roughly larger than the size of a hair, use a pencil or garden marker to gently remove a single plant from the mass and transplant it into the garden. Space onion sets 3–6 inches apart on the row. Several rows of onions can be planted on top of a 4-foot row or bed. I've seen up to 5 rows, but for an increased bulb size, I recommend limiting 4-foot beds to 3 rows each.

Typical Number of Plants on a 10-Foot Row

On a typical 10-by-4-foot row, expect 40–180 onions. The larger the number and the less space provided per plant, the smaller the bulb.

Plant Spacing in a Container

Plant up to 10 onion sets per 5-gallon container. The closer the plant spacing, the smaller the mature bulb.

Typical Fertilizer Requirements

In raised beds and in-ground gardens, apply a complete fertilizer such as 13-13-13 to the soil at a heavy rate one to three weeks prior to planting. Water in immediately. Side-dress onions three weeks after planting and again three weeks later. At each side-dressing, apply two teaspoons of a 15% nitrogen fertilizer between every third bulb or plant. Water in immediately.

To side-dress onion sets in a 5-gallon container, mix 1 tablespoon of a water-soluble 15% nitrogen fertilizer into a gallon of water. Pour the fertilizer solution into the container; avoid wetting the foliage. One gallon of solution is plenty of fertilizer to use per side-dress application. If the container is extremely wet, break this application into 2 applications 3–4 days apart.

Insects of Concern

Thrips.

Diseases of Concern

Purple blotch, downy mildew, pink root.

Harvest Time

Onions are generally harvested when 50% or more of the foliage has fallen over. Simply pull the onions from the soil and cut the tops about 1 1/2 to 2 inches above the bulb. Keep in a dry, dark, cool area. Allowing onions to dry for a week under a carport or in a covered outdoor space with a fan blowing on the harvest will greatly increase storage life and reduce noxious odors in your home.

A Brief Glance: Onions

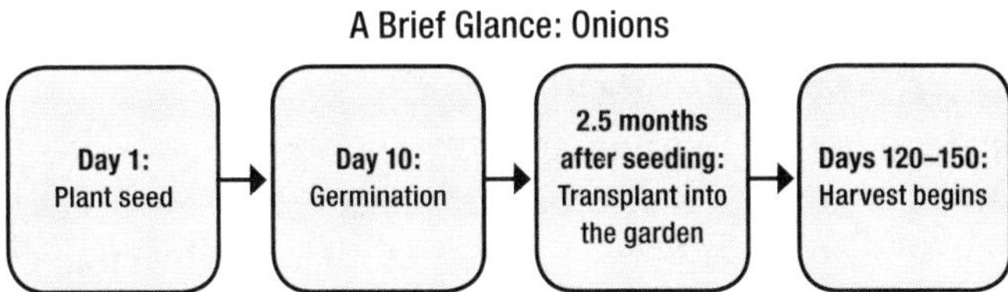

General Comments

Purchasing thick onion sets from a nursery in December does not necessarily mean bigger bulbs earlier. Larger sets tend to grow faster, and with the onset of a freeze or hard frost, they will bolt (go to flower/ seed) and not set a bulb. Since the goal is to eat onions and not make seed, start with smaller sets.

Onions can take up to 200 days from seeding to producing a bulb. Be patient. Many gardeners get anxious when they see that bulbs are sticking up above the soil line but the foliage has not yet fallen. Don't go out and start breaking the foliage. It will fall naturally. Breaking the foliage may induce disease and early rot. Allow this crop time to start drying on its own.

SHALLOTS

Planting Dates

Plant shallot bulbs directly into the garden from July through February.

Plant Spacing

Space shallot bulbs 6–8 inches apart and 1 inch deep. Plant toes point side up by simply pushing into the soil. You will not need tools if the ground is well prepared.

Typical Number of Plants on a 10-Foot Row

20–30 shallot plants.

Plant Spacing in a Container

Plant up to 6 shallot bulbs per 5-gallon container. Thin often to keep bulbs from crowding each other out and reducing plant quality.

Typical Fertilizer Requirements

In raised beds and in-ground gardens, apply a complete fertilizer such as 13-13-13 to the soil at a heavy rate one to three weeks prior to planting. Water in immediately. Side-dress shallots when foliage is 6 inches high and again at 12 inches. After you harvest and separate bulbs, replant again into the garden bed and side-dress upon replanting. At each side-dressing, apply one teaspoon of a 15% nitrogen fertilizer per plant.

To side-dress shallots in a 5-gallon container, mix 1 tablespoon of a water-soluble 15% nitrogen fertilizer into a gallon of water. Pour the fertilizer solution into the container; avoid wetting the foliage. One gallon of solution is plenty of fertilizer to use per side-dress application. If the container is extremely wet, break this application into 2 applications 3–4 days apart.

Insects of Concern

Thrips.

Diseases of Concern

Downy mildew.

Harvest Time

Shallot foliage can be broken from the plant at any time and used to season food. Harvest shallot bulbs when the plants have become giant masses of foliage, generally 12 inches or so wide. Consume the foliage and bulbs but save a few back and immediately replant into the garden. Continue to do this throughout the planting season. Generally, the last crop of shallots is harvested in May. At this time, the remaining bulbs are consumed or processed for long-term storage. Save a few bulbs back and dry them in a covered outdoor area. Then store in a cool, dry location until you plant again next season.

A Brief Glance: Shallots

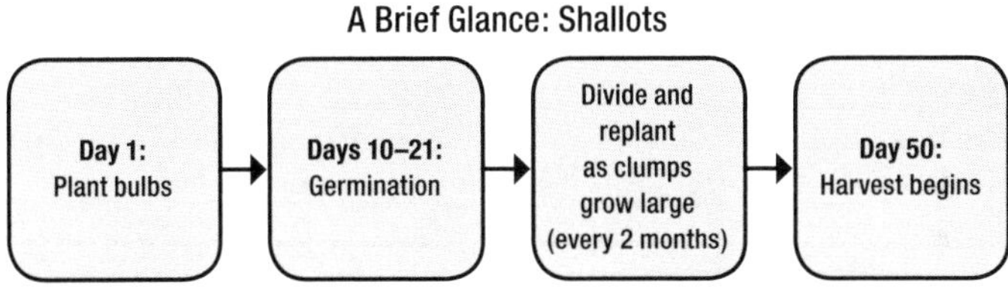

General Comments

Shallots are a nice addition to the garden. Plant them if you are seeking a more garlic-flavored onion top. Both the foliage and the bulbs are edible.

Many varieties of shallots were once available on the market. But since these prized crops have been traded so freely among home and commercial gardeners, there is no telling what type you are planting.

South Louisiana was at one time a major producer of commercial shallots. But as higher-paying, less backbreaking jobs became available, labor became a problem for the producer. Now shallots are grown as specialty items on some farms and in many home gardens.

Family Chenopodiaceae

Chenopodiaceae is actually a subfamily within the family Amaranthaceae. There are so many plants in this family they deemed subfamilies necessary. Normally gardeners think of the Amaranthaceae as amaranth or pigweeds . . . and generally these are thought of as weeds in a vegetable garden. Chenopodiaceae is also termed the Goosefoot family. It received this rather silly name because if you really use your imagination, the foliage of many of these plants resembles a goose foot.

BEETS

Planting Dates

Fall beets

Direct seed beets into the garden mid-August through October.

Spring beets

Direct seed beets into the garden mid-January through late February.

Plant Spacing

Space beet seed 2–4 inches apart and no deeper than 1/4 inch into the soil.

Typical Number of Plants on a 10-Foot Row

It is hard to determine the total number of beets that can be planted on a 10-foot row. You'll need less than 1/4 ounce of seed to broadcast seed across the row/bed top. The farther apart you space beets, the larger they will become, generally maxing out at 4–5 inches in diameter. Like other root crops, beets are not necessarily better when larger.

Plant Spacing in a Container

Scatter beet seeds into the top 1/4 inch of soil in the container. Thin plants to 2–6 inches apart depending on how large you desire the beetroot.

Typical Fertilizer Requirements

In raised beds and in-ground gardens, apply a complete fertilizer such as 13-13-13 to the soil at a medium rate one to three weeks prior to planting. Water in immediately. Make sure this fertilizer is banded approximately 4 inches below the soil line or, if you plan to broadcast seed into the garden area, wait a week after fertilizing before direct seeding this crop. Side-dress beets three weeks after planting with one teaspoon of a 15% nitrogen fertilizer per plant. Water in immediately.

To side-dress beets in a 5-gallon container, mix 1 tablespoon of a water-soluble 15% nitrogen fertilizer into a gallon of water. Pour the fertilizer solution into the container; avoid wetting the foliage. One gallon of solution is plenty of fertilizer to use per side-dress application. If the container is extremely wet, break this application into 2 applications 3–4 days apart.

Insects of Concern

Aphids, flea beetles.

Diseases of Concern

Cercospora leaf spot, downy mildew, damping off.

Harvest Time

Beets can be harvested very small—from the size of a quarter up to 5 inches across. Don't wait too long or the root will start to crack. Beet foliage can also be consumed; toss it into a salad for color and additional flavor.

A Brief Glance: Beets

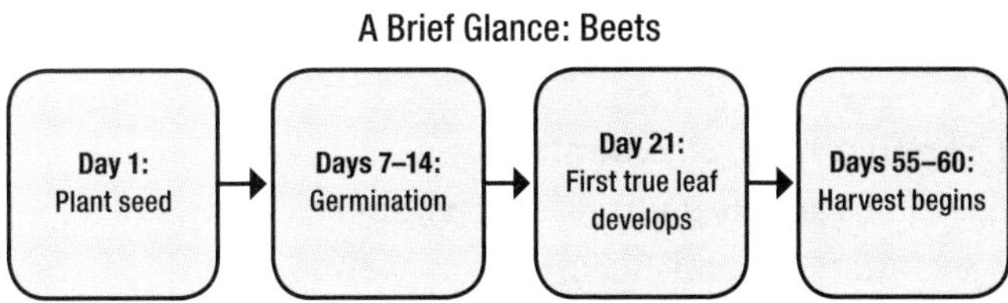

General Comments

Not only do beets have culinary purposes, but they can be used in crafting as well. After boiling beets for your meal, use the hot water to tie-dye shirts, socks, and handkerchiefs for children.

Having trouble getting your beet seed to germinate? The soil may be too warm. Wait until temperatures have cooled to plant seed or start seed in a wet paper towel in the refrigerator. Keep the seeds in the fridge for 24 hours and then carefully plant into the garden.

CHARD

Planting Dates

Fall chard

Direct seed or transplant chard seedlings into the garden mid-August through the end of October.

Spring chard

Direct seed or transplant chard seedlings into the garden mid-January through early May.

Plant Spacing

Space chard plants 6–8 inches apart. Be careful when direct seeding not to plant too thick so you will not waste plantlets later when thinning to 6–8 inches apart.

Typical Number of Plants on a 10-Foot Row

Up to 22 plants on a double-drilled row.

Plant Spacing in a Container

Plant 3 or 4 chard seedlings per 5-gallon container.

Typical Fertilizer Requirements

In raised beds and in-ground gardens, apply a complete fertilizer such as 13-13-13 to the soil at a medium rate one to three weeks prior to planting. Water in immediately. Make sure this fertilizer is banded approximately 4 inches below the soil line or, if you plan to broadcast seed into the garden area, wait a week after fertilizing before direct seeding this crop. Side-dress chard two weeks after planting and again three weeks later. If you direct seeded chard, make sure foliage is at least 3–4 inches tall prior to the first side-dress application. At each side-dressing, apply one teaspoon of a 15% nitrogen fertilizer per plant. Water in immediately.

To side-dress chard in a 5-gallon container, mix 1 tablespoon of a water-soluble 15% nitrogen fertilizer into a gallon of water. Pour the fertilizer solution into the container; avoid wetting the foliage. One gallon of solution is plenty of fertilizer to use per side-dress application. If the container is extremely wet, break this application into 2 applications 3–4 days apart.

Insects of Concern

Aphids, grasshoppers, snails and slugs, flea beetles.

Diseases of Concern

Cercospora leaf spot.

Harvest Time

Harvest chard leaves when they are 4–12 inches tall. The entire plant can be removed by cutting at the soil line, or you can simple pull outer leaves of the plant, allowing it to slowly rejuvenate. But once the weather has warmed or gotten extremely cold, the plant will bolt and the foliage will become bitter.

A Brief Glance: Chard

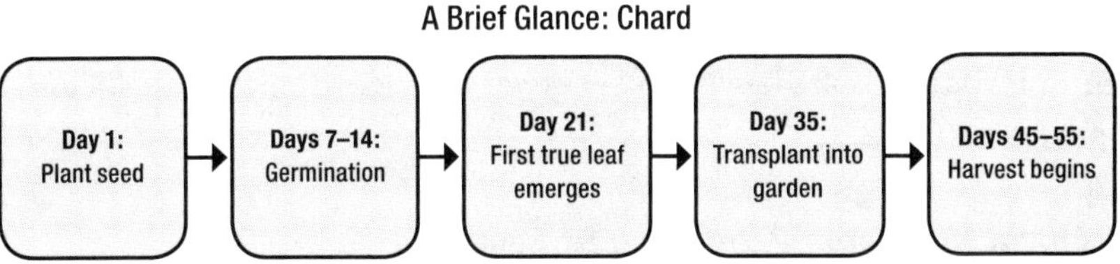

General Comments

In addition to being a tasty vegetable crop, chard gives gardens a bright pop of color. The main stem can range from white to various shades of orange, yellow, pink, and red. One of the most beautiful varieties is Bright Lights. Some gardeners strip the foliage from the stems for consumption, while others eat the stems too. Imagine celerylike texture when consuming the stems. Chard can be eaten raw, cooked like greens, or even baked into a healthy chip alternative.

Don't wait too long to harvest and enjoy chard. Yes, it is pretty, but the purpose of this plant is to be eaten! Plant a few extra seedlings in your ornamental beds to enjoy the bright colors for a longer period of time.

SPINACH

Planting Dates

Fall spinach

Direct seed into the ground as soon as soils start to cool. Because Louisiana has unpredictable temperatures, it is really hard to say how early one can begin planting spinach—typically not until late September and only then if the weather has cooled off. Direct seeding can continue through mid-November.

Early spring spinach

Direct seed into the garden from mid-January through February.

Plant Spacing

Space spinach seed 3–6 inches apart. Try mixing seed with sand or shaking from an old spice container to achieve a more even stand. Seed should be planted only twice as deep as it is wide, so no deeper than 1/8 inch into the soil. Try pressing the seed into the soil and then watering in, or if your soils are heavy in clay, cover with loose potting media instead of native soil.

Typical Number of Plants on a 10-Foot Row

One packet is more than enough seed for a 10-foot row of spinach as 1/4 ounce can easily cover 100 feet of row.

Plant Spacing in a Container

Direct seed spinach into the top 1/4 inch of soil in the container. Thin plants to at least 3 inches apart as they emerge.

Typical Fertilizer Requirements

In raised beds and in-ground gardens, apply a complete fertilizer such as 13-13-13 to the soil at a medium rate one to three weeks prior to planting. Water in immediately. Make sure this fertilizer is banded approximately 4 inches below the soil line or, if you plan to broadcast seed into the garden area, wait a week after fertilizing before direct seeding this crop. Side-dress spinach two weeks after planting and again three weeks later. I also side-dress spinach after the first and second harvests to encourage foliage to flush out again and again. At each side-dressing, apply one teaspoon of a 15% nitrogen fertilizer between every other plant. Water in immediately.

To side-dress spinach in a 5-gallon container, mix 1 tablespoon of a water-soluble 15% nitrogen fertilizer into a gallon of water. Pour the fertilizer solution into the container; avoid wetting the foliage. One gallon of solution is plenty of fertilizer to use per side-dress application. If the container is extremely wet, break this application into 2 applications 3–4 days apart.

Insects of Concern

Aphids, caterpillars, snails, slugs.

Diseases of Concern

Anthracnose, bacterial leaf spot, downy mildew.

Harvest Time

Harvest spinach leaves when they are 6 inches high or shorter. I harvest spinach the same way as mustard and turnip greens: Cut off all of the foliage except for the bottom 2 or so inches, immediately side-dress, and water in. The foliage will flush out easily a second and third time. To avoid having too much spinach ready at one time, consider successional plantings.

A Brief Glance: Spinach

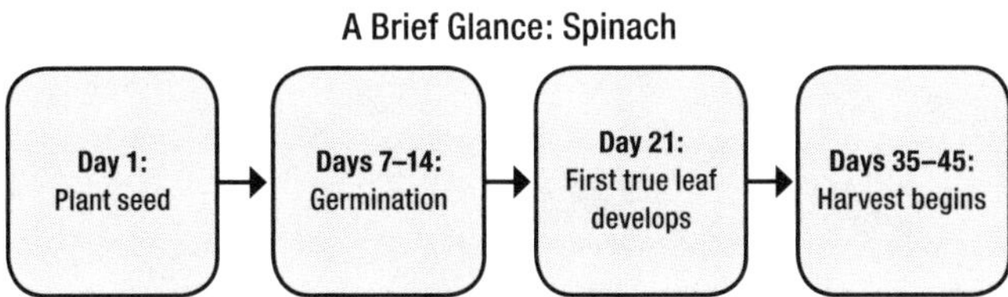

General Comments

Germination of spinach seed can be difficult. If you can't wait for the soil to cool, try this trick: Place the seed in a damp paper towel and keep in the refrigerator for 24 hours, and then sow into the ground. The cold temperatures help the seed germinate. It is also critical that spinach seed not used in the current planting season be stored in a refrigerator or freezer. Doing so will prolong the shelf life of the seed.

This quick crop is sure to please the impatient gardener as it can be harvested in as little as 35 days given proper care and environmental conditions.

Spinach should definitely be part of every fall garden. Not only because it is so tasty, but because it is really good for you too! Try spinach in salads, cooked with meats, added to casseroles, as a pizza topping, or blended into smoothies.

Family Apiaceae

Members of this family include carrots, celery, parsnips, and several common herbs such as parsley, cumin, dill, and cilantro. Many members of the family Apiaceae are known for their taproots.

CARROTS

Planting Dates

Fall carrots

Direct seed carrots into the garden early September through early November.

Spring carrots

Direct seed carrots into the garden mid-January through mid-February.

Plant Spacing

Space carrot seed 1–2 inches apart and no more than 1/8 inch deep. Carrot seed needs some light to germinate. Planting any deeper will prevent germination.

Typical Number of Plants on a 10-Foot Row

It is hard to determine a typical number of carrots on a 10-foot row. It depends on how well the gardener spaced seed or thinned plants, and if rows are planted or if seed is broadcast across the row/bed or in the container.

Plant Spacing in a Container

Direct seed carrots into the container. Thin seedlings to at least 1–2 inches apart when they are 3–4 inches tall.

Typical Fertilizer Requirements

In raised beds and in-ground gardens, apply a complete fertilizer such as 13-13-13 to the soil at a medium rate one to three weeks prior to planting. Water in immediately. Side-dress carrots when they are roughly 6 inches tall.

Whether they are growing in gardens or containers, it is easiest to side-dress carrots with a water-soluble fertilizer. Mix 1 tablespoon of a water-soluble 15% nitrogen fertilizer into a gallon of water. Pour the fertilizer solution into the container; avoid wetting the foliage. One gallon of solution is plenty of fertilizer to use per side-dress application. If the container is extremely wet, break this application into 2 applications 3–4 days apart.

In a raised bed or in-ground garden, continue to make batches of fertilizer solution until you have drenched one side of the carrot row(s) throughout the garden.

Insects of Concern

Aphids, whiteflies.

Diseases of Concern

Rot, downy mildew, southern blight.

Harvest Time

Carrots are generally harvested 70–80 days after planting when the top portion of the taproot is showing slightly above the soil line. Carrots may be harvested earlier than this for a tender and less crisp taste. But if you are growing colored carrots other than orange, it is best to wait until they are fully mature for optimum color development.

A Brief Glance: Carrots

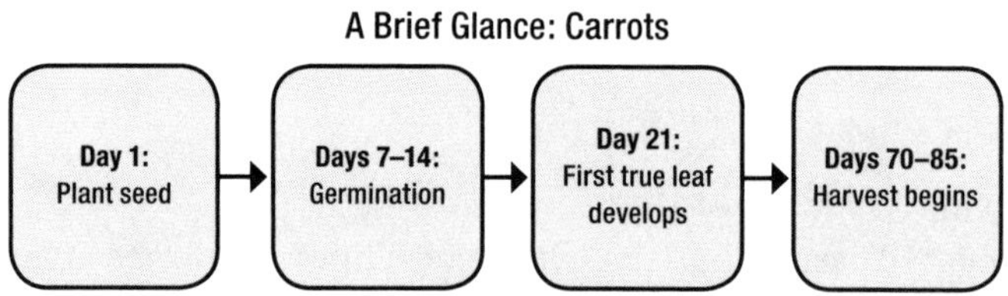

General Comments

Carrots come in many colors. Try growing ivory, yellow, orange, red, and purple carrots to brighten your fall and early spring harvests.

Leave tops of carrots on for children so they can eat like Bugs Bunny.

Want straight, long carrots? Till the soil at least 6–8 inches deep or grow carrots in loose media in containers and raised beds. Any pebbles, rocks, or chunks of clay will act as a barrier to the carrot's growth. Instead of growing through these obstacles, they will split and grow around them, causing forked or nubby carrots.

There are shorter-variety carrots such as Little Finger, but carrots are all slim and pointy. The baby carrots you see in the grocery store have been mechanically shaped to give that rounded short stature.

Although we mentioned a few potential pests, carrots are an easy crop to grow, provided they are not sitting in saturated soil.

Thyme

COMMON GARDEN HERBS

Herbs make a wonderful addition to any edible garden for a variety of reasons:

- If allowed to bloom, herbs attract pollinators to the garden.
- Herbs add a soft texture to a vegetable garden, helping increase its aesthetic appeal.
- Seasoning vegetables with freshly grown herbs enhances flavor without negatively impacting health. Many herbs can be substituted for butter and salt to add flavor to almost any recipe.

There are many types of herbs that can be grown in Louisiana. This book covers those that are easiest to grow.

What is the difference between an herb and a spice? An herb and a spice may come from the same plant, only different portions. Herbs are edible foliage and stems, whereas spices are edible seeds or roots. For example, the herb cilantro is the leaves and stems of the cilantro plant, and the spice coriander is the seeds of the same plant. When ginger root is dried and ground, it becomes a spice.

Warm-Season Herbs

BASIL

Grow basil plants in conjunction with tomatoes. Basil is one of the main ingredients in pesto.

Plant basil transplants or seeds into the garden in the spring when the soil warms. Space transplants 12 inches apart. If you decide to direct seed this crop, plant the seed no more than 1/4 inch deep. Basil will readily reseed itself throughout the season, and with mild winters you have an increased chance of small basil seedlings returning when the weather warms.

The edible portion of this plant is the foliage. Keep the foliage pinched back to maintain a bushy plant that doesn't bloom. Once the basil plant begins to bloom, its focus shifts from foliage production to seed production and the plant will complete its life cycle. To extend harvest, keep the foliage pruned.

MINT

Nothing is better than walking through the garden with an ice-cold glass of lemonade or sweet tea flavored by a fresh sprig of mint.

Mint can be direct seeded into the garden when soil temperatures are around 70°F—mid- to late March. Transplants can be planted into the garden about one foot apart from one another during the spring and summer months. Once you plant mint, you will never be without it. This hardy plant just doesn't give up! In fact, it spreads. If you are gardening in a small space and want to have room for other edibles, consider planting mint in a pot to control spreading.

There are many types of mint: regular, spearmint, chocolate, pineapple, and so on. Try a few types and see what your family likes best. As with other herbs, pinch back flower blooms to extend harvest.

ROSEMARY

Rosemary is a warm-season herb treasured for its flavor as well as its evergreen beauty. This perennial shrub is an excellent addition to any edible or ornamental garden.

Rosemary is almost always transplanted into the garden. This can be done year-round, but the rosemary will have a better chance of survival if planted in the early spring or early fall. There are two types of rosemary, trellising and bush. Foliage of both is edible. This shrub can become huge, towering 8 feet tall and nearly as wide if not pruned. Space plants at least 4 feet apart. Prune as often or as little as you desire. You can prune rosemary into topiary shapes or leave it alone for a more natural look. One plant is plenty for a family, but most gardeners plant more because it adds a touch of evergreen to the garden.

THYME

Thyme is a warm-season herb commonly planted into gardens in the spring. Space plants 18 inches apart or direct seed into the garden, pressing the seeds into the soil. Light is required for germination. Regularly clip back foliage to extend the harvest season.

Cut sprigs of fresh thyme to enhance the flavor of most vegetable side dishes and fish.

Cool-Season Herbs

CILANTRO / CORIANDER

Cilantro is a cool-season herb, although it is a staple ingredient in "hot" Latin dishes.

Cilantro can be direct seeded or transplanted into the garden. Direct seed in the early spring (early March), when soil temperatures are close to 65°F, and plant no deeper than 1/4 inch. Transplants can be planted throughout the spring season, or plant seeds again in the fall (September). Space plants 6–10 inches apart. This is a bushy plant that can reach mature heights of 2 feet. If you let it go to flower, you will now be producing the spice coriander.

DILL

Another cool-season annual herb, dill is popular not only with humans but with the black swallowtail butterfly as well. If you notice lots of larvae swarming the foliage, don't worry; they will soon turn into beautiful butterflies . . . but you might need to plant more dill for yourself.

Direct seed dill when the soil temperatures are cool, around 60°F (late February–early March), and again in the early fall (September). Dill seed requires some light for germination. Therefore, do not plant too deep, or simply press seed into the top of the soil and water in with a breaker on the hose to prevent seeds from washing off the top of the row.

Dill also transplants well from small seedlings in both spring and fall. Make sure to space at least one foot apart as these plants can become quite large. Dill foliage and seeds are popular for pickling cucumbers and other vegetables. To extend harvest, pinch back flower buds and maintain a bushy plant.

OREGANO

A cool-season herb popular for combining with homegrown tomatoes to enhance the flavor of Italian dishes, oregano is one herb you'll need in the garden.

Oregano is generally transplanted into smaller gardens in the early spring (February) or early fall (September). If you are seeding, do so when the soil is cool (around 70°F) and make sure that the seed is exposed to sunlight. Simply press the seed into the soil and lightly water with a hose attached to a breaker or water wand. Space oregano plants 24 inches apart.

PARSLEY

This cool-season annual is popular with Cajun chefs. It is commonly added to soups, stews, and gumbos just before the dish is removed from the stove or chopped and sprinkled fresh on top of étouffée, rice and gravy, and other Cajun comfort foods.

Parsley is most commonly planted into small gardens by transplants in the early spring (February–March) and again in the early fall (September). However, if you plan to start this herb from seed, plant the seed no more than 1/4 inch deep and when soils are cooler (65°F). Parsley grows as tall as it does wide, averaging 8 inches to 2 feet in diameter. Space plants accordingly.

WRAPPING UP

I hope this book has provided you with all of the information you need to start growing a small urban/backyard/home garden. If there is just one piece of advice I can emphasize, it is to start small and grow your garden larger as you gain experience. This is especially true for the first-time gardener as well as those who have given up because of past failures. There is nothing wrong with gardening in a single container. Starting small produces confidence. Understanding what works in your own yard and then growing larger is key to success. Most of the successful gardeners I know did not plow up an acre one day . . . they started with a plant or two, a container, or one small raised bed, and have gradually dedicated more and more space to their home, school, and community gardens. The tips below in conjunction with starting small are the take-home notes I hope you will remember. So now that the research (reading) portion is over, start your own garden experiment and just have fun with it!

Tips to Garden By

1. *Invest time into your soil.* Taking soil samples every three years and applying the recommended amounts of nutrients through organic or synthetic means to achieve optimum plant production is important. Just as important is ensuring that the soil is worked, or tilled, so that plant roots can easily grow and maneuver through the soil. This is true no matter if you are growing directly in the ground, in a raised bed, or in a single container.

2. *Start with healthy plants.* Discounted vegetable transplants were probably not watered correctly, have insect troubles, or are already showing symptoms of virus or disease. Don't fall for a plant discount. Start robust and healthy and end with success.
3. *Space plants properly.* Providing a little extra room will go a long way to limiting insect and disease occurrence in the garden.
4. *Water at the base of plants.* Do you pour drinks on your arm? No, because that's not an efficient way to hydrate your body. Plants "drink" from their roots, where the majority of the water will be taken up and used for plant growth. The only time to water plants on their foliage is when they are *severely* wilted or if you are applying one specific micronutrient as a foliar spray to the plant. An example would be applying Solubor, or boron, to broccoli to avoid a purpling of the foliage and to reduce incidence of hollow stems.
5. *Stake and trellis where needed, and limit direct contact of soil on produce.* Not all crops need to be staked, but for those that do (tomatoes, pepper, eggplant, etc.), this is an important step not to skip. Some crops do better with but don't require staking (cucumbers, pole beans, extra-large asparagus plants). Without trellising where needed, you can guarantee almost immediate rot of sensitive fruits touching the ground. When sunlight is blocked from one side of the fruit, normal ripening is distorted. Also, there are many good and bad microorganisms living in the soil that would like a bite of that tomato or eggplant as much as you. Not to mention the soil is where snails and slugs hang out, and they will quickly take advantage of your hard work. So pull vines up on a fence line, invest in cages, or build your own creative trellis out of materials you have on hand. I've even seen one school repurpose an old soccer goal as a trellis for their Malabar spinach!
6. *Mulch around the base of plants.* Mulch, like trellising, provides a protective layer between the nasty creatures in the soil and your produce. It also helps keep crops like lettuce and spinach free from grit when you are enjoying your homegrown salad. In addition to these benefits, mulch helps retain soil moisture, regulates soil temperatures, and prevents some weed seed from germinat-

ing. Mulching is always a good idea. Recommended mulches for vegetable crops include pine straw, leaves, newspaper, plastic manufactured mulch, weed-barrier cloth, and shade cloth.

7. *Practice patience.* Vegetable crops, even the quick ones (radishes: 28 days from seed to harvest), don't grow overnight. While you certainly do not want to neglect your garden, over-nurturing by applying too much water or fertilizer can stress plants out. If you feel like your garden is not growing, take a weekend trip. You'll be pleasantly surprised by the growth over just a three-day period. Read the seed packages and stake labels when you purchase your vegetables. Mark on a calendar the approximate time you should be harvesting these crops so you can more accurately gauge how well the garden is doing. But remember, each backyard throughout Louisiana is like a small niche, and each will grow at its own rate depending on soil health, protection from cold, amount of sunlight, disease and insects present, and other factors. With time, you will learn how your garden functions in relation to typical standards provided for gardens in the Deep South.
8. *Create a garden journal.* You will be surprised at how helpful it is to keep a journal to help you remember year after year which varieties performed the best and which vegetable crops just do not do well in your soil. Journaling will remind you when to plant and approximately how long it takes to harvest the crop, so you'll become a more efficient gardener by just flipping through your old garden journal. Important items to record include planting dates, variety names, planting locations (especially if you have multiple gardens or a very large garden), pests you noticed, dates you fertilized, and environmental conditions such as rain and average temperatures.

APPENDIX
LOUISIANA GARDENS WORTH VISITING

Many locales in Louisiana have herb, fruit, or vegetable gardens open for public viewing. Check out the websites for the gardens and organizations listed below before making a visit—many have limited hours of operation or entrance fees. Some have other features of interest, such as historic homes or restaurants, that will make your visit even more enjoyable. Please do not pick produce at any of the community gardens listed below.

Audubon State Historic Site
11788 Hwy 965/P.O. Box 546
St. Francisville, LA 70775
http://www.crt.state.la.us/louisiana-state-parks/historic-sites/audubon-state-historic-site/index

Avery Island
(Tabasco—McIlhenny Company)
http://www.tabasco.com/avery-island/
During pepper season, this island boasts not only the beautiful Jungle Gardens but also many acres of tabasco pepper fields. Avery Island is located just south of New Iberia.

Botanic Garden at Independence Park
7950 Independence Blvd.
Baton Rouge, LA 70806
http://www.brec.org/index.cfm/page/380

Chef John Folse's White Oak Plantation
17660 George O'Neal Rd.
Baton Rouge, LA 70817
http://whiteoakplantationbr.weebly.com/

Good Food Project of the Food Bank of Central Louisiana in partnership with the Central Louisiana Community Foundation
(community garden network in the Alexandria area)
3223 Baldwin Ave.
Alexandria, LA 71301
http://www.goodfoodprojectcenla.org/site/Home.aspx

Hollygrove Market and Farm
8301 Olive St.
New Orleans, LA 70118
https://hollygrovemarket.com/

Houmas House Plantation and Gardens
40136 Hwy 942
Darrow, LA 70725
http://houmashouse.com/gardens.htm

Iberia Community Garden
1505 South Hopkins St.
New Iberia, LA 70560
https://www.facebook.com/iberiagardencoop/info/?tab=overview

Ira Nelson Horticulture Center
2206 Johnston St.
Lafayette, LA 70503
http://inhc.louisiana.edu/

La Provence: A Chef John Besh Restaurant
25020 U.S. 190
Lacombe, LA 70445
http://laprovencerestaurant.com/

Laurens Henry Cohn Sr. Memorial Plant Arboretum
12206 Foster Rd.
Baton Rouge, LA 70811
http://www.brec.org/index.cfm/park/CohnArboretum

LSU AgCenter Botanic Gardens at Burden
4560 Essen Lane
Baton Rouge, LA 70809
http://www.lsuagcenter.com/portals/our_offices/research_stations/botanic-gardens

New Orleans Botanical Garden
1 Palm Drive
New Orleans, LA 70124
http://neworleanscitypark.com/botanical-garden

Parkway Partners
(community garden network in the New Orleans area)
1137 Baronne St.
New Orleans, LA 70113
http://parkwaypartnersnola.org/

Windrush Gardens
(separate garden housed in the Burden Museum and Gardens)
4560 Essen Lane
Baton Rouge, LA 70809
http://www.lsuagcenter.com/portals/burden/windrush-gardens/

INDEX

MY GARDEN NOTES